Dear Maureen,

Look forward to seeing you i Ibi
soon.

Regards

Ajeet Basaj

Snow Leopard Adventures,
Sept 2008.

TREKKING
IN THE
HIMALAYA

TREKKING
IN THE
HIMALAYA

Text: **Hashmat Singh** ▲ **Pallav Das**

Photographs: **Hashmat Singh**

Maps: **Jai Kumar Sharma**

Lustre Press
Roli Books

ISBN: 81-7436-106-5

Text: © Hashmat Singh and Pallav Das 2002
Photographs: © Hashmat Singh
Design: Sneha Pamneja

Third impression 2005
© Roli & Janssen BV 2002
Published in India by
Roli Books in arrangement
with Roli & Janssen BV
M-75 Greater Kailash-II (Market)
New Delhi 110 048, India.
Phone: ++91-11-29212271, 29212782
Fax: ++91-11-29217185
Email: roli@vsnl.com
Website: rolibooks.com

Printed and bound in Singapore

■I Preceding pages 2-3: Camp below Dzongri ridge
in the Kanchenjunga region, western Sikkim
■I Following pages 6-7: Camp below Dhankar
gompa beside the Spiti river

Contents

▮I The trail in the upper Tirthan valley in Kullu, Himachal

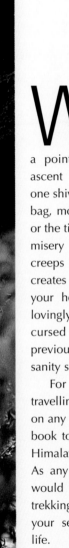

The First Step

'Because it was there'
— George Mallory
on why he climbed Everest

WHY does one wander about in the hills? Why does one trudge up steep slopes only to descend to a point where another formidable ascent stares mockingly? Why does one shiver endlessly in a thin sleeping bag, most inappropriate for the place or the time, only to wake up to further misery as the late night rain finally creeps through the tent floor and creates a dreadful little puddle near your head? And why does one so lovingly plan another trek after having cursed and howled through the previous one and questioned one's sanity sixteen times a day?

For the answers, armchair travelling just won't do. You have to go on any one of the treks detailed in the book to find out why trekking in the Himalaya is so insidiously addictive. As any self-respecting street peddler would tell you, you just have to try trekking to feel what it could do to your senses, your world-view, your life.

Trekking is not about the challenge and the triumph of scaling that brutally tough 26,248 ft / 8,000 m-plus mountain through that complicated route that nobody has dared before. It's not about that glorious placard which attaches itself to your back, screaming 'conqueror' as you descend to base camp. Trekking, in fact, is about that bracing bonfire which spirals up to meet the stars. It's about pitching camp overlooking a stunning waterfall. It's about standing transfixed on that rock outcrop as you look at the golden eagle glide past the precipice, breaking the symmetry of the trans-Himalayan vistas, and swooping down on the unsuspecting mountain hare. It's about lying down on a carpet of anemones next to a gurgling stream. It's about stopping the knees from shaking after you have just been rescued by an obliging porter from a narrow ledge where loose rocks were giving way in a hurry. It's about feeling envious of those climbers who haughtily march past you like zombies, totally focused on that awe-inspiring peak another 10,000 ft / 3,045 m above you _ you could get closer to that only by using your long telephoto lens. And after being overwhelmed by everything around you, it's about looking inwards and remembering and then trying to forget the pain of the journey.

The five regions that comprise the trekking heartland of the Himalaya are: Ladakh/Zanskar; Himachal; Garhwal/Kumaon; Sikkim/Darjeeling; Nepal and Bhutan.

We will take up each region and discuss in detail the day-by-day itinerary of the treks. Once you are through with this book, we hope you will be fortified by your newly-gained wisdom to try at least a few of the treks. This book is a modest attempt at presenting the attractive possibilities of trekking in the Himalaya and at expressing the characteristics of various regions in terms of flora, fauna, geological features, cultural diversity and environmental pressures. It's an attempt at letting the sweet whiff of the pine cones reach you and help you to dig out those dusty hiking boots from the cupboard. Have fun!

■I Hashmat Singh, the author, in front of Lingshi Dzong, Bhutan

Trip Grading

1 Easiest. These involve just a few days of walking over easy trails and no difficult elevation gain or high pass crossings.

2 Easy to Moderate. These treks include hiking over easy, but high passes that require acclimatisation.

3 Moderate. The treks are longer in duration and involve a fair amount of elevation gains and losses, high campsites and pass crossings.

4 Moderate to Rigorous. Such treks have elevation gains and losses of 2,500 to 4,000 ft / 760 to 1,220 m on some days, six to seven hours of hiking at times and the occasional difficult and high pass crossing.

5 Rigorous. Include treks with very high campsites – over 14,000 ft / 4,267 m – and several very high pass crossings of over 16,000 ft / 4,875 m, with some days of up to ten to eleven hours of hiking.

The Trekking Guide

A hundred years ago you could not have journeyed in the Himalaya without being an experienced traveller, ready to take risks. Today the situation is much changed, with tourism playing a vital role. However, the Himalaya still form the boundaries of many nations and the political situation in most is still a matter of concern. Travel plans must be made keeping this in mind. Then there is the need to be physically and mentally prepared and to think ahead when planning. Having said that, the famous English explorer, Eric Shipton, could organise his expeditions to the Himalaya 'in half an hour at the back of an envelope'!

Today's styles of trekking

Make sure you like hiking in the first place! Then consider some short hikes nearer home to develop basic fitness. Consider carrying a backpack, camping for days together, walking on rough trails, the different foods, the language barrier, and the time you can allot to trekking. This will help you to select the trek best suited to you.

Walking alone or with a few friends can be wonderful, though it is easier for the young as you need to put more than walking into your day. If you plan to camp out and cook, develop stamina. If you plan to stay in local homes or teahouses, then you must know the language a little. Be prepared for smoky rooms, lice and fleas, and crying babies. Also to be considered are difficult-to-find trails. Carrying all your gear can be the most tiring way to walk in the mountains, so you could **make arrangements with a local porter or (and) a guide** who will help you find your way and procure food and shelter. Making your own arrangements can be daunting. It might be prudent to approach a **local tour operator** for the task. Most operators also provide equipment, making it unnecessary to carry or buy large tents and sleeping bags.

Travelling with a group arranged by an operator from your home country is often favoured these days. Such group travel is organised by the foreign tour operator through a local operator. A leader who is versed with the local language and culture accompanies the groups. The tour operator can be held responsible if all the services promised are not delivered, as you will be protected under the laws of your home country. This is important in an area where it is not unusual to be offered far more than is finally delivered. The downside is that such tours offer no flexibility: the groups stick to an itinerary; exploring alone or mixing with the locals is limited.

Preparation for the trip

There are various factors to consider, both mental and physical, in preparation for the trip:
• Physical conditioning of the cardiovascular system with aerobic exercise.
• Background reading, maps etc.
• Passport, visas, restricted area permits, travel and evacuation insurance, etc. Each country in this region has a different set of visa requirements and travel restrictions that keep changing. Often the visas and permits must be acquired in your home country, well before the travel dates. After reaching your destination, it is extremely difficult to acquire them.

You are the final judge of what you may need, but it is no good to be burdened with baggage. On a typical trek day it can be very warm during the day, yet below freezing at night. Often, washing can be difficult since only cold water is available; drying of clothes could take several days.

Clothing and personal gear

When planning what to take, do consider the following:
• Clothing must be cool and loose fitting, easy to wash and dry,

so that walking becomes easy.

• Clothing made of materials that wick sweat easily like polypro or capalene.

• Several layers of warm clothing are preferable to one thick layer.

• Very good quality **rain gear.**

• Excellent quality medium to lightweight **trekking boots** that are well broken in.

• Sun protection like sun cream, a wide-brimmed hat, sunglasses, lip balm, moisturisers.

• Medical kit (**see separate section**), toilet kit, a flashlight (torch).

Camping and cooking equipment

This depends on the style of trekking, but if you are totally equipping yourself then you could consider the following:

• **Sleeping bag** with liner and foam mattress.

• Sturdy **rain-proof tent**.

• Backpack, day pack and probably a duffel bag to keep in storage in hotels while on trek.

• A kerosene stove that can be cleaned easily, a leak-proof fuel container. Lightweight pots, pans and cutlery. Favourite food items.

Miscellaneous

Keep this to a minimum: a notebook and pens, reading and information material, pocket knife, water bottle (essential) with water purification tablets, tampons or sanitary napkins, umbrella, camera and film (difficult to get while on trek), extra batteries, repair kit with duct tape, rubber bands, quick drying 'super' glue.

Postscript: You would not get very far if you have to carry everything. Reduce this list to what suits you. If you have lots of baggage, hire a porter and enjoy the trip.

Medical guidelines

Despite the low level of medical aid in the mountains, the chances of a trekker being taken seriously sick are not very high. But, perfectly healthy people have often suffered because of pushing themselves when they shouldn't have and not anticipating what they were getting into. Basic precautions before the trip include **physical conditioning, a medical check-up, relevant immunisations**, and having **a portable medical kit**.

Altitude sickness

No other mountains deserve the kind of respect the Himalaya do in terms of altitude. As the Himalayan Rescue Association likes to point out: 'The Himalaya start where other mountains leave off.' Remember it is the sleeping altitude that is critical. Acclimatisation depends on 1) the altitude; 2) the rate of ascent to that altitude, and 3) susceptibility to altitude sickness. Men and women are equally susceptible and children more so.

The way to prevent altitude sickness is to give the body enough

time to get used to the rarefied air. **A slow and steady ascent is vital**. **Adequate hydration** is also helpful. The body is constantly losing fluid from the lungs and the skin in the high, dry environment. Drink enough to maintain a clear and abundant urine output. Other measures include eating a **high carbohydrate diet**, climbing high during the day and coming lower down to sleep, and to do mild to moderate activity during the day rather than just lie around.

The drug of choice for altitude is **Acetazolamide (Diamox),** a sulpha drug. It hastens acclimatisation, increases breathing, reduces alkalinity and diuretic fluids. The usual regimen is 125 to 250 mg twice a day, starting 24 hours before ascent, and continuing through the first 24 hours at altitude. Almost all altitude problems can be avoided if symptoms are recognised and acted upon. The warning signs are: headache, lack of appetite, nausea, feeling of tiredness, and sometimes

vomiting. This stage of mild mountain sickness can be treated with aspirin or Diamox for headache and something mild for the nausea and vomiting. When these first symptoms appear, stop ascending. If they persist, then descend as soon as possible. If there is trouble with co-ordination, change in consciousness or evidence of fluid in the lungs, descend immediately. If these symptoms are developing then the person is heading for **Acute Mountain Sickness (AMS)**. The single most reliable sign is loss of co-ordination. Other symptoms are recurrent vomiting, severe headaches, hallucinations, loss of interest, paralysis, seizures, and unconsciousness. This type of AMS is called High Altitude Cerebral Oedema (HACE).

Another type of AMS is High Altitude Pulmonary Oedema (HAPE). It can often result in death, caused by fluid accumulating in the lungs. Early recognition of symptoms – a dry cough, low ability to exercise and excessive breathlessness, and rapid heartbeats during exercise – is again the key. As symptoms develop, there could be breathlessness even at rest; the fingernails may turn bluish or grey, and a gurgling sound may be heard in the lungs. A few hours before death, the cough would become wet and produce pink, frothy sputum. Immediate descent is the only answer.

The trekker's medical kit

The suggested list includes prescription items, so **consultation with a physician is necessary**.

- *If crossing malarial areas:* Malarial prophylactics and mosquito repellent.
- *Wound disinfectant*: Betadine.
- *Blister treatment*: Moleskin, second skin or cloth adhesive tape.
- *Adhesive strips*: Band-aids in different sizes.
- *Gauze pads and rolls:* elastic bandage.
- *Thermometer*
- *Analgesics:* Aspirin or Tylenol, Tylenol with codeine.
- *Anti-inflammatory*: Ibuprofen
- *Antibiotics:* Ciprofloxacin, Bactrim DS or Septra DS, Erythromycin, Gentamycin eyedrops, any skin antibiotic
- *Anti-diarrhoels*: Lomotil, Pepto-Bismol, Imodium.
- *Anti-nausea drugs*: Pheregan, Compazine
- *Antihistamine:* Benadryl
- *Decongestant:* Sudafed
- *For high altitude*: Diamox

■I A glowing Everest stands tall amidst an ampitheatre of icy white and steep darkness

2
' A Circle of White Fire '

THE Himalaya, one of the most spectacular creations of nature, are actually a part of a continuum that stretch from present-day Uzbekistan and Khirgizstan in the west to Myanmar in the east. The Hindu Kush, Pamirs, Tien Shan, Kun Lun, Karakoram, and the Himalaya merge into one another as if in secret conspiracy. This swath of ice has inspired astronauts to declare that 'the mountain complex of central Asia illuminates the heart of the continent like a circle of white fire'. Within this circle, each range has evolved to acquire a unique character.

Today, it is difficult to imagine that the Tethys sea ruled supreme from the Hindu Kush to the Arakan ranges. Around eighty million years ago when dinosaurs were vanishing, Laurasia and Gondwanaland were the two land masses in the north and the south respectively, with the Tethys sea in between. Laurasia then divided into Europe-cum-Asia and North America-cum-Greenland; Gondwanaland subdivided into five regions: Africa, India, Australia, South America, and Antarctica. Except for India, these four slowly came to their present positions. Within fifty million years, India steadily moved northward until it smashed against Asia. The Indian landmass pushed the soft underbelly of Asia with cataclysmic energy, giving rise to this great chain of mountains.

The most identifiable footprint of the collision was Lato, a small village in Ladakh on the Manali-Leh highway, and the first point of the collision. Jagged, wafer-thin cliffs dominate Lato. Elsewhere, in the adjoining region of Spiti, the rocks have imprints of sea waves and embedded marine fossils. In the bazaars of Spiti you can even pick up fossilised molluscs and ammonites. A fossilised hippopotamus skull was found at 14,000 ft / 4,865 m in Ladakh in 1991.

The history of Himalayan explorations has been written by disparate people – army commanders like Alexander, Genghis Khan, Taimur Lane, and Babur; seekers of knowledge like Huien Tsang and Fa Hien; explorers like Marco Polo; early Jesuits trying to spread Christianity; East India Company officials; British army officers; Survey of India explorers in the garb of pilgrims, and others like scientists, naturalists, hunters, adventurers, and mercenaries. The Himalaya beckoned everybody who thought he had a chance against the mountains, a discovery to make and a story to recount upon return. Many perished, some disappeared and a few became legends in their lifetime. Through perseverance, desire and greed, the Himalaya were laid open, and stories and information, sometimes credible but mostly fantastic, began emerging.

■I Top and facing page: Tsarap Lingshi valley in Zanskar

At the end of the nineteenth century, the focus shifted to the pinnacles. Man was finally pushing the limits of his endurance and character. After climbing the major peaks of the Alps by the mid-nineteenth century, the European mountaineer looked for greater heights. The Royal Geographical Society of London extended its patronage to mountaineering and in 1892, it sponsored a expedition to the Karakoram, led by Martin Conway, an experienced alpinist. The expedition surveyed the Baltoro Glacier; several major peaks were discovered and triangulated, and

Pioneer Peak (22,600 ft / 6,888 m) was climbed — the greatest height that man had set foot on. The Duke of Abruzzy, Alexander Kellas, George Mallory, Andrew Irvine, Maurice Herzog, Eric Shipton, Bill Tilman, Tom Bourdillon, Bill Murray, and John Hunt opened up new routes to the Himalaya. The French reached the summit of Annapurna in Nepal in 1950, the first (26,248 ft / 8,000 m) peak to be climbed. In 1951, Eric Shipton found a route to the south face of the Everest and in 1953 Tenzing Norgay and Edmund Hillary, climbed it.

This was just the beginning. A

major Indian expedition in 1965 put nine people atop the south summit, the largest for one expedition, and ten years later, Junko Tabei, a Japanese, became the first woman to climb Everest. Since then Reinhold Meissner, an intrepid Austrian climber, has been to the top of all the 26,248 ft / 8,000 m peaks without oxygen, and Sundare Sherpa of Nepal has climbed the Everest thirteen times! The new trend is to organise small alpine-style expeditions. Solo climbing is popular. With people setting up personal targets, sometimes verging on the absurd, the charm of the early days of

God gulps down the sea

A HINDU myth has it that Lord Vishnu swallowed up the sea so that a pair of seagulls could lay their eggs on the land thus created. This tale provides the mythological parallel to the disappearance of the Tethys sea. For the Aryan settlers in the Indo-Gangetic basin, the Himalaya or the Abode of Snow was an object of veneration. Much before it became fashionable and politically judicious for the Western explorer to make forays into the Himalaya, the Indian pilgrim had already probed its recesses. He was searching for the sources of the great rivers and the mythical mountains, for locations to put up sacred shrines, and for salvation. The pilgrim cut across the Great Himalayan Range to reach Tibet, to explore the regions around the sacred Mount Kailash, because he realised that this was the fountainhead from which the four great rivers (the Indus, Sutlej, Ganges, and Brahmaputra) of the subcontinent flowed. Thus, the symbolism behind Mount Kailash as the abode of Lord Shiva is based on the realisation that these rivers have sustained civilisations and the homeland.

climbing has disappeared. With commercialisation, the approach routes to peaks look like public parks on a Sunday. As a result, the mountains are coming under pressure and may not take it for long.

But away from the pursuit of personal glory lies the mysterious yet fulfilling charm of trekking and hiking. Trekking does provide the ideal combination of exploration, leisure, and sport to the jaded post-modern psyche. But as ecological concerns over the Himalaya gain support, the need for toning down the assault mentality is felt acutely. People need to come to the mountains, but their intervention should be minimised to sustain the ecosystem.

▌I Probjika Valley in central Bhutan

3
Secret Bhutan and Sikkim-Darjeeling Wonderland

THERE are very few places left in the world that evoke the kind of mystery as does the kingdom of Bhutan. Given its geographical isolation and its strictly controlled tourism policy, people have often taken recourse to wild flights of fancy. But then, in Bhutan, it does become difficult to distinguish fact from fantasy. Swirling clouds and mist obscure and reveal by turns the hilltop monasteries framed against the backdrop of lofty sacred mountains. The mythical flaming dragons and flying tigers come alive, compelling the mighty warriors and holy monks to emerge from the wall paintings to overpower the beasts and restore order.

In Bhutan, history and mythology exist together. Archaeological evidence suggests that a pastoral society had come up in Bhutan as early as 2000 B.C. As in the rest of the Himalaya, traditions of the animistic Bon religion guided the life of the early inhabitants till the second century A.D. when Buddhism filtered into this area. Change came in the eighth century when Guru Padmasambhava, the renowned Indian teacher, made visits to Bhutan. Buddhism became an inseparable part of the life and consciousness of its people. Known all over the Himalayan Buddhist world as Guru Rimpoche or the Precious

Master, Guru Padmasambhava set up many monasteries all over Bhutan.

The medieval history of Bhutan was shaped by developments in Tibet. Denominational conflicts within Buddhism often caused turmoil. Drukpa Kagyu or the Thunder Dragon sect established in the eleventh century in the Tibetan town of Ralung, faced constant persecution from the Gelug-pa sect. This led Tibetans to migrate to Bhutan and the Drukpa sect spread over the region. Ngawang Namgyal, a charismatic figure of the seventeenth century, unified the country through a subtle mix of diplomacy, alliances, and brute force. He extricated Bhutan from the political domination of Tibet and set up fortress monasteries – the *dzongs* – which performed civil, religious, and defensive functions. Taking on the title of Shabdrung or The Precious Jewel at Whose Feet One Prostrates, Ngawang

Namgyal repelled Tibetan attacks and quelled rebellion within Bhutan, ushering in peace and prosperity.

The growing influence of the British in India also had its impact. Within Bhutan the Shabdrung's position was challenged, and in 1907, Bhutanese chiefs and lamas elected Ugyen Wangchuk as the hereditary ruler. He maintained good ties with the British as did his successors with India after Independence.

The Bhutanese monarchy has been cautious in opening up the country. Tourists, other than Indian citizens, are allowed into the country only through officially recognised travel agents, and $200 per day is charged during the peak season from March to June. Off-season discounts are available.

Landlocked between Tibet and India, Bhutan is a mountainous country ranging in altitude from 328 ft / 100 m in the south to the 24,785 ft / 7,554 m Kulha Kangri Peak on the Tibetan border. The northern-most part of Bhutan is an area of glacial peaks and high valleys, snowbound for the greater part of the year. The bulk of the population lives in Thimpu, Paro, Ha, and Samtse in the west, and Bhumthang and Trongsa in central Bhutan. These valleys form the area richest in natural wealth.

....

Trek I   Paro-Lingshi-Thimpu

■l Thimpu, the seat of the Bhutanese monarchy

Ways & Means

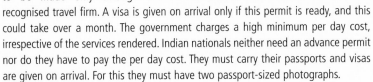

Duration
10 days

Degree of Difficulty
4: Moderate to rigorous

Permits
Entry into Bhutan for foreigners is restricted and arrangements have to be made only through a recognised travel firm. A visa is given on arrival only if this permit is ready, and this could take over a month. The government charges a high minimum per day cost, irrespective of the services rendered. Indian nationals neither need an advance permit nor do they have to pay the per day cost. They must carry their passports and visas are given on arrival. For this they must have two passport-sized photographs.

Getting There
Paro is the only airport and there are flights by Druk Air from Bangkok, Kathmandu, Kolkata, and Delhi. By road, Paro is linked to India from the border town of Phuntsholing, and is eight hours by bus. From Paro to the road head at Drugyal Dzong is only an hour's drive.

Best Time
Mid-March to mid-May and September to mid-December. Early snows by end-November could block passes and late monsoons could make the trails muddy.

Altitude
The trek starts from Drugyal Dzong at 8,465 ft / 2,580 m. The high passes are Niyela La at 16,000 ft / 4,877 m, and Yale La at 15,800 ft / 4,815 m.

Highlights
Excellent views of peaks like Jomolhari, Jichu Drake, and Tserim Kang from many sections; the remote monastery at Lingshi; thick spruce and mixed rhododendron forests in the latter half of the trek.

Support Services
All services like trekking equipment, cooking, and porterage are provided by agents of a government-recognised travel agency. Very few facilities are available. Be totally self-equipped from Paro or Thimpu.

Emergency
Air rescue available only under extreme cases. The climatic conditions in Bhutan are unpredictable, making rescue extremely difficult. On this trek, Lingshi is the only place you can communicate from.

The drive through Paro valley from the airport is all that Bhutan is about. It is a wide, open, undulating valley stretching out in inviting green for miles. The day could be spent relaxing in a hotel or acclimatising by going on a short hike to a *dzong*. You can go to Taksang or the Tiger's Nest monastery, located on the cliff-top and built in the eighth century. Guru Padmasambhava is credited with its establishment. The legend goes that he flew on a flaming tigress to the top of this mountain to set up the monastery. Given its location, you will also wish that you could fly there. Tourists cannot go beyond a point and have to satisfy themselves with a distant but stunning view. In fact, all over Bhutan, the sanctum sanctorum of any monastery is off-bounds. Special permission is required but rarely granted. Only the courtyard may be visited.

■ DAY 1: The trek starts with a drive to the right bank of the Paro Chhu river. Drugyal Dzong (8,465 ft / 2,580 m), in ruins, is at the end of the road. There the ponies are loaded up. The sacred peak of Jomolhari beckons but its vanilla cone disappears for the next few days. You enter an idyllic pastoral setting – charming little

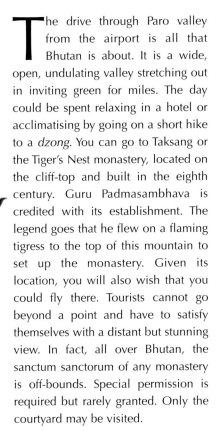

Paro-Lingshi-Thimpu

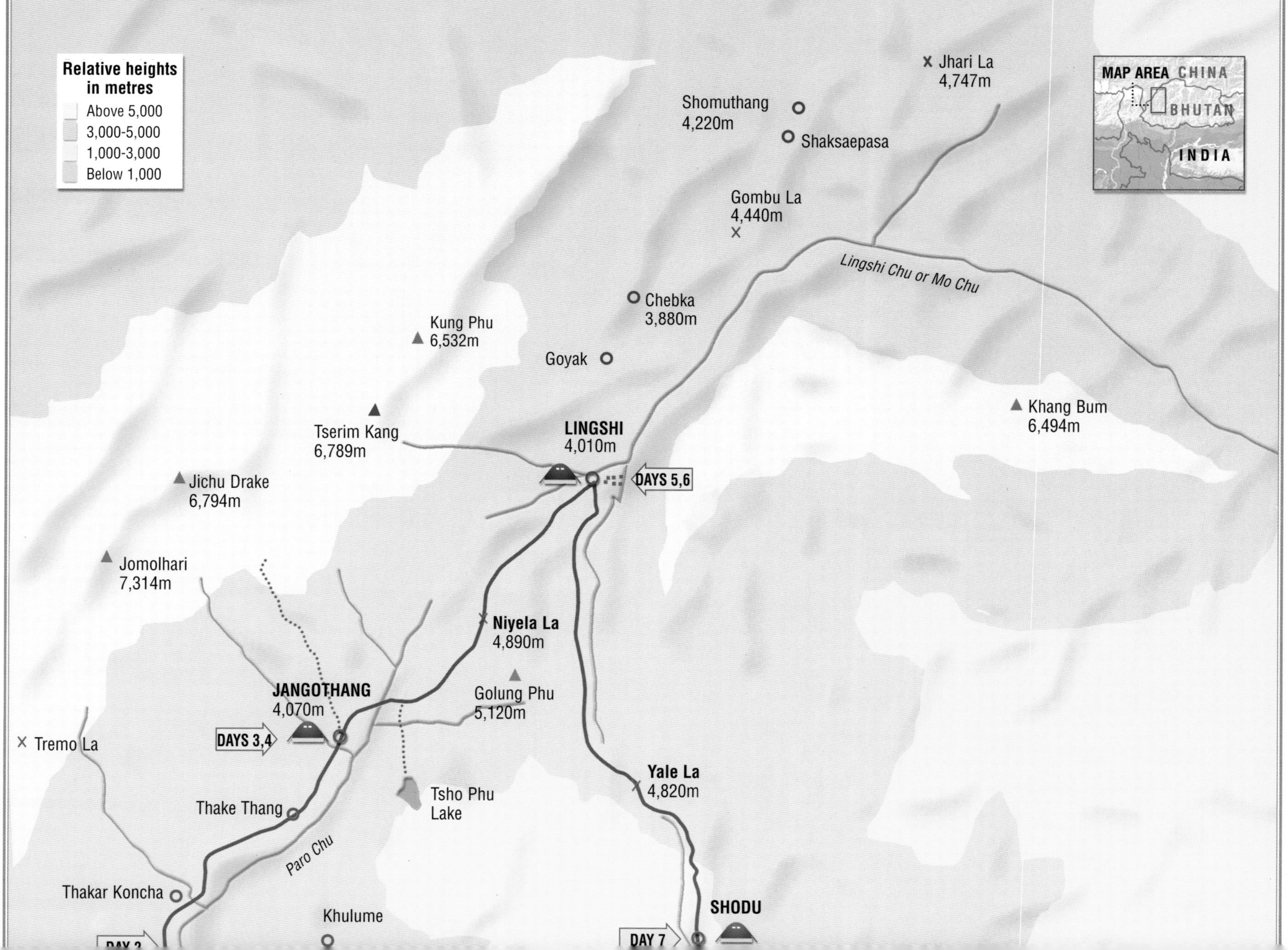

Relative heights in metres
- Above 5,000
- 3,000–5,000
- 1,000–3,000
- Below 1,000

MAP AREA
CHINA
BHUTAN
INDIA

× Jhari La
4,747m

Shomuthang
4,220m

○ Shaksaepasa

Gombu La
4,440m ×

○ Chebka
3,880m

Lingshi Chu or Mo Chu

Khang Bum
6,494m ▲

Goyak ○

Kung Phu
6,532m ▲

Tserim Kang
6,789m ▲

LINGSHI
4,010m

DAYS 5,6

Niyela La
4,890m ×

Golung Phu
5,120m ▲

Tsho Phu
Lake

Yale La
4,820m

SHODU

DAY 7

Jichu Drake
6,794m ▲

Jomolhari
7,314m ▲

JANGOTHANG
4,070m

DAYS 3,4

Thake Thang ○

Pao Chu

Khulume ○

× Tremo La

Thakar Koncha ○

DAY 2

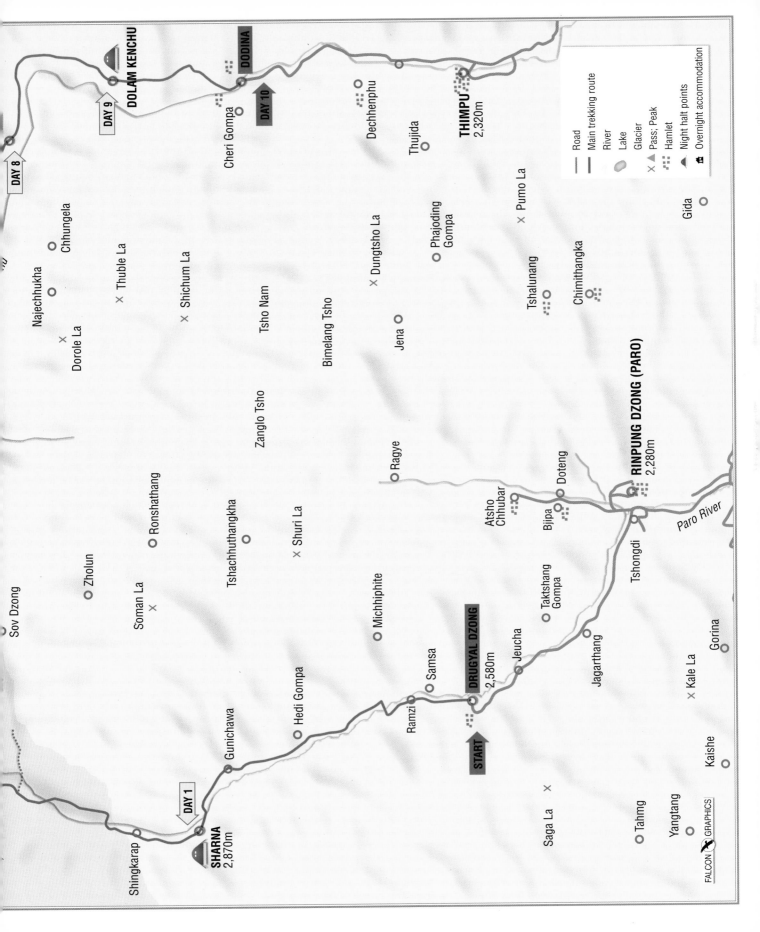

■I Rinpung Dzong in Paro valley. On the hill is Ta Dzong, which houses the premier museum of Bhutan.
■I Facing page: A bridge over Nikka Chu river near Rukubji village, central Bhutan

houses in the middle of green fields with the backdrop of wooded hills. An hour up the trail you reach a suspension bridge to cross over to the left bank. The trail enters a pine forest after going past three *chortens*. Walking for two hours, you reach a Bhutanese Army camp at Sharna (9,416 ft / 2,870 m), where permits are checked. Crossing over to the right bank, set up camp in the meadows.

■I **DAY 2:** A two-hour climb through a forest leads to a clearing called Shingkarap that has a small house and a farm. Half an hour from this clearing lies a tricky fork that could send you to Tibet! Follow the track downhill and right for thirty minutes to cross over to the left bank of the Paro Chu, and to the meadow of Thangdo Zam. A steep two-hour climb brings you to another river bridge that leads to the right bank. Soon the valley takes a left turn. A hard thirty-minute climb leads to the Thang Thanka meadow (11,910 ft / 3,630 m). Two huts mark this place, and it makes for a kitchen during the night halt.

■I **DAY 3:** After a half-hour climb you reach the meadow of Thakar Koncha. Another steep thirty minutes bring you to a *mane* wall (stone wall with inscriptions), which signals the start of the yak herders' camp. Climb for another two hours to reach the yak herders' camp at Thake Thang that overlooks the ruins of a fortress. The trail plateaus out and takes you to the meadow of Jangothang (13,353 ft / 4,070 m) at the base of Jomolhari. A small valley to your left leads to the base camp.

■I Yaks on Dholum Kenchu meadow

sight of the Jichu Drake peak, if you are willing to follow the ridge for an hour. It can be windy though.

o Going up the valley for an hour or so will also get you great views of Jomolhari and Jichu Drake from a different angle. This is also the next day's route.

o A nearby high-altitude lake gives you the possibility of fishing. Take a guide for this walk.

■I **DAY** 5: The trail climbs for forty-five minutes and descends to the river. Crossing the river, it climbs to Niyela La (16,044 ft / 4,890 m). A false hump only increases the torture as you come up to do the last one hour of the energy-sapping scree. But it's worth it. The top of the pass has views of Jomolhari, Jichu Drake, and Tserim Kang. Look straight ahead: the serpentine Mochu river shimmers. Below, Lingshi Gompa is balanced on a hillock; to your left, Tserim Kang and Jichu Drake straddle an imposing glacier. Descending for ninety minutes through forests, you reach the camp.

■I **DAY** 6: Take a rest. Or choose to limber up to see the monastery of Lingshi (13,157 ft / 4,010 m). There are huge pastures up from Lingshi on the ridge towards Tserim Kang and a high-altitude lake too. This is ideal blue sheep and musk deer country.

■I **DAY** 7: The trail climbs down to the Mochu river. The Lingshi Dzong is

■I **DAY** 4: Take a rest. The ponies go back and the yaks from Lingshi arrive. Go for any of these short walks:

o A ridge walk that gives you a great view of the two glaciers and a grand close-up of Jomolhari and Tserim Kang. You also get a spectacular

behind you, framed now in the foreground of the Kung Phu (21,000 ft / 6,400 m). Go through noisy marmot country on the ascent to Yale La. A three-and-a-half-hour ascent along the Mochu takes you to its top. Walking over boggy grounds, three peaks – Jomolhari (23,997 ft / 7,314 m), Jichu Drake (22,291 ft / 6,794 m), and Tserim Kang (22,275 ft / 6,789 m) – come into view for the last time. A slow descent for ninety minutes brings you to a large flat meadow. It is a deceptively pretty place that is windy and does not make for a campsite. A forty-five-minute descent brings you to the turn-off to Shodu (13,225 ft / 4,030 m), marked by a *chorten*. The place is just above the tree line at the headwaters of the Thimpu Chu and is a good campsite.

■I **DAY** 8: Morning time, the trail leaves the open country to enter a thick cypress forest mixed with juniper and rhododendrons. The first hour is through boggy grounds. This is great pheasant country if you have time to scout. After criss-crossing the Thimpu Chhu, the last one hour of a steep climb takes you to the ruins of Barshong Dzong. Just ahead is a steep meadow that makes for a camp. But you will have to look for a dry spot.

■I **DAY** 9: Begin a never-ending search for a place called Dolam Kenchu, which in Bhutanese means 'well short'. Which is just as well because as you start inching your way towards it, you will feel that you cannot reach it. All the resting places on this day are called Dolam Kenchu. Confusion reigns. The trail descends steeply through a cypress

■I Niyela La with Jomolhari and Jichu Drake; below: Lingshi Dzong; facing page, bottom: takin, Bhutan's national animal

forest for the first two hours. Keep your eyes open for this is a typical eastern Himalaya bird paradise. A slow three-hour ascent brings you, finally, to Dolam Kenchu (11,200 ft / 3,414 m). Yet, as the name suggests, you are still well short of the destination.

■I **DAY 10**: Just a day away from Thimpu. The trail initially ascends to a small pass (11,000 ft / 3,353 m). It then descends steeply to the road-head village of Dodina (8,400 ft / 2,560 m) through a forest of conifers and oak. You walk through an elegant traditional wooden bridge thatched with bamboo.

▌I Kanchenjunga (in the background) illuminated by the late evening sun

The Wonderland

Twelve kilometres away from Darjeeling is Tiger Hill. From there you can see the Everest and other giants, but Kanchenjunga is the reigning queen. For ages the drama of pink turning into mauve, orange, and scarlet has left many a schoolboy rooted to the ground. The promise is that it shall continue to do so for those who venture up the Teesta valley.

Darjeeling or the Hill of the Thunderbolt (*dorje* refers to a thunderbolt and *ling* to a place in Tibetan) belonged to Sikkim and was fought over for between the Nepalese and Sikkimese. In the 1830s, the British, looking for a respite from the humidity of Kolkata, negotiated a deed with the Maharaja of Sikkim for what they called 'a worthless uninhabited mountain' to exploit its 'sanatorial possibilities'. The British had obviously seen the importance of Darjeeling's location, providing ready access to Nepal and Bhutan, and opening up trading avenues for the East India Company. By 1857, Darjeeling became the official summer seat and a thriving town. The characteristic British hierarchy was also on display. Prominent citizens lived on higher grounds. As the altitude decreased, so did the social standing of the inhabitants.

The British influence did not spread too far into the rest of Sikkim, but politically the region did become a part of the British empire by 1890.

Lepchas, who today form 18 per cent of the population, were the original inhabitants. They are thought to have migrated to Sikkim around the thirteenth century from the Assam hills. That probably explains the origin of the word Sikkim (New House), in the Tibetan language.

Squeezed in between the two kingdoms of Nepal and Bhutan, the Sikkim-Darjeeling region is a geographical wonderland. Dominated by a rugged topography, its two main mountain ranges are the razor-edged Singelila range on the western border, with Nepal and the Chola range on the eastern border with Tibet. These structures form a near impregnable barrier. The low-altitude Pangola range separates Sikkim from Bhutan. South of Darjeeling, undulating low ridges take you to the Bengal plains. On the western border lies Kanchenjunga, the third highest peak in the world at 28,168 ft / 8,585 m, presiding over a court of at least ten peaks above 20,000 ft / 6,095 m. Through this region runs another ridge which

■I The interior of the Lhakhang in Rumtek Gompa

separates the Teesta and Rangeet rivers.

For ages, passes have been used for trade, war, religious, and cultural exchange and travel. Chiwanhangjang Pass (10,300 ft / 3,140 m) on the Sikkim-Nepal border was used by the Nepalese to attack Sikkim during the nineteenth century. Through this pass waves of immigrants made their way into Sikkim. As a result, the Nepalese today form 75 per cent of the population. On the eastern Chola range, the two vital passes between Sikkim and Tibet are the Nathu La and Jelep La. The Indian and Chinese troops face each other at Nathu La, scene of a 1962 Sino-Indian battle.

The most important attraction, however, has been Kangchendzonga (the local term for Kanchenjunga), or the Snow Castle of the Five Treasures. Kanchenjunga is easily visible from a great distance. On a clear day it can be seen from Siliguri in the Bengal plains as one entrains for Darjeeling. Only low foothills separate it from the plains, and these cannot protect it from the fury of the south-west monsoon. The result is a yearly precipitation of snow greater than in any other Himalayan peak. The snow plasters itself on the mountain and fills up every crack with ice. This ice breaks off in chunks hundreds of feet thick and falls thousands of feet in

avalanches. These are Kanchenjunga's weapons against the mountaineer. So much so that it took fifty years to reach the top. The first attempt was made in 1905. But it was only in 1955 that Kanchenjunga was climbed by a British expedition. The climbers stopped short of the summit in deference to Sikkimese feelings. That has been the practice since.

For the mountaineer and the trekker, the Kanchenjunga region is a near-mystical experience. You do not lay siege to the mountain; you let the elements take you as high and as far as possible. Then you return with the memory of one of the most incredible images of the infinite on earth.

Trek I   Kanchenjunga Base Camp

For a hiking enthusiast setting foot in the eastern Himalaya for the first time, it is but natural to choose the Kanchenjunga Base Camp trek. Not taking this trek is like missing out on the Taj while sight-seeing in Agra.

Alighting from the plane at Bagdogra Airport or from your train at the Siliguri railway station, drive off in the direction of Kanchenjunga and reach the trek road head at Yoksum in eight hours. Or take the detour to Darjeeling. This hill station is coming to terms with the thick coat of dust on its once gilded frame. Darjeeling was once known throughout the British Empire as the Queen of the Hills. The best way to reach Darjeeling is via the *toy train* from Siliguri. The train service was started in 1881. It plods along, faithful to the tempo of that era: the ninety kilometre journey takes eight hours. After reaching Ghoom, the highest point on the trek, the train begins a hurried descent to Darjeeling town.

The place for soaking in the allure of that era is Windamere Hotel. Many expeditions must have been planned in the hotel drawing room where tea is still served to the strains of the string quartet. There is enough to occupy you in Darjeeling: The planter's club – to check out what the *burra sahibs* did in their leisure time; the plantations, to look at the best tea in the world, the monasteries during the daytime and the bazaars in the evening.

Yoksum is reached in eight hours

of driving. It's a pleasant drive, first down the Teesta valley to the confluence of the Teesta and Rangeet rivers, and then along the Rangeet to the Yoksum. Its present status belies its historical significance. It was the capital of the kingdom, and the Nyingmapa order of Tibetan Buddhism was set up there. Yet, Dubdi *gompa* (a monastery) is just a forty-minute walk from Yoksum.

At Yoksum, hotels with eateries are good for trekkers on limited budgets. Sikkim Tourism also maintains tourist huts all through the route and you do not need tents. However, higher up, the huts do not offer individual rooms and are bare but sturdy. For those carrying tents, there are camping sites all along the route.

As the day after the arrival at Yoksum is spent making trek preparations, go for short forest walks. Those interested in bird-watching would be richly rewarded. Laughing thrushes, black-headed sibias, grey and red-headed tits, red-billed blue magpies, black and white-cheeked *bulbuls*, shortwings, and various kinds of flycatchers can be seen with little effort.

▌ **DAY 1:** You have two options. With tents, you can pitch a camp at the Prek Chu bridge – a five-and-a-half-hour walk from Yoksum. If living in a tourist hut, then walk another steep one-and-a-half hours to reach Bakhim. Considering that Bakhim is at 8,800 ft / 2,682 m, you would have

Duration: 10 days

Degree of Difficulty
4: Moderate to rigorous

Getting There
Direct regular flights from Delhi and Kolkata to Bagdogra (near Siliguri); a five-hour drive from Darjeeling, and a ten-hour drive from Yoksum, the road head. Trains also run to Siliguri.

Best Time
April to end May; October to mid-December.

Altitude
The highest altitude reached is atop the Gocha La, 16,208 ft / 4,940 m.

Highlights
Spectacular views from Dzongri ridge and Gocha La pass of the Kanchenjunga massif.

Support Services
Porters and mules available at the road head at Yoksum but it takes time to arrange for them; food not available – only basic rations can be had at Yoksum, so carry them from Darjeeling; huts on the way can be used for sleeping, but carry your own camping equipment.

Emergency
No communication facilities or medical services anywhere on the trek.

▌ Blood pheasant

Kanchenjunga Base Camp

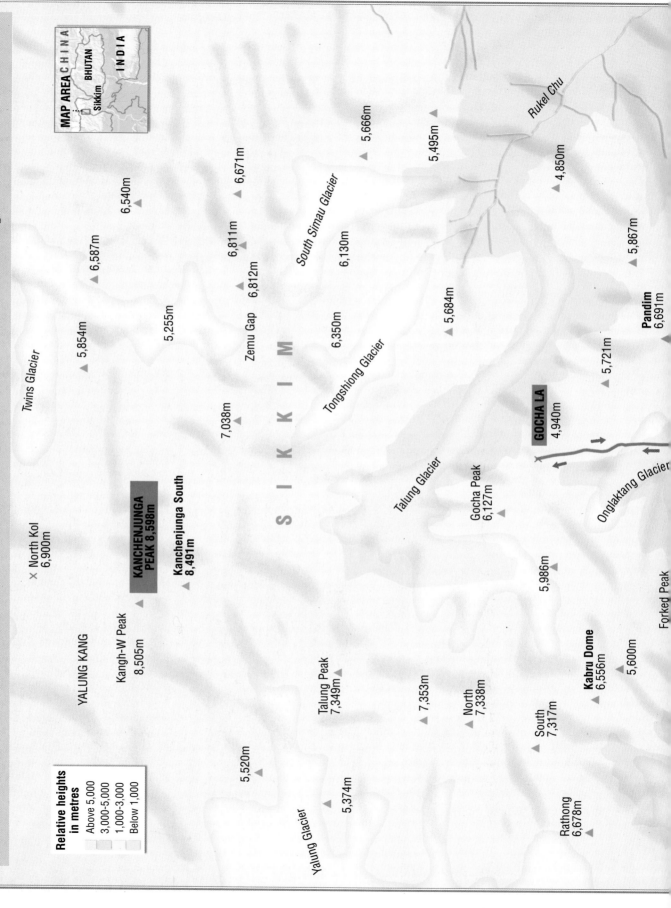

MAP AREA
CHINA
BHUTAN
Sikkim
INDIA

Relative heights in metres
Above 5,000
3,000–5,000
1,000–3,000
Below 1,000

Twins Glacier

North Kol
6,900m

YALUNG KANG
Kangh-W Peak
8,505m

KANCHENJUNGA PEAK 8,598m

Kanchenjunga South
8,491m

5,854m

6,587m

6,540m

5,255m

6,671m

6,811m

6,812m
Zemu Gap

7,038m

South Simau Glacier
6,130m

5,666m

5,495m

4,850m

Rukel Chu

5,867m

Pandim
6,691m

6,350m
Tongshiong Glacier

5,684m

5,721m

GOCHA LA
4,940m

Onglaktang Glacier

Talung Glacier

Gocha Peak
6,127m

S I K K I M

Yalung Glacier

5,520m

5,374m

Talung Peak
7,349m

7,353m

North
7,338m

South
7,317m

5,986m

Kabru Dome
6,556m

5,600m

Forked Peak

Rathong
6,678m

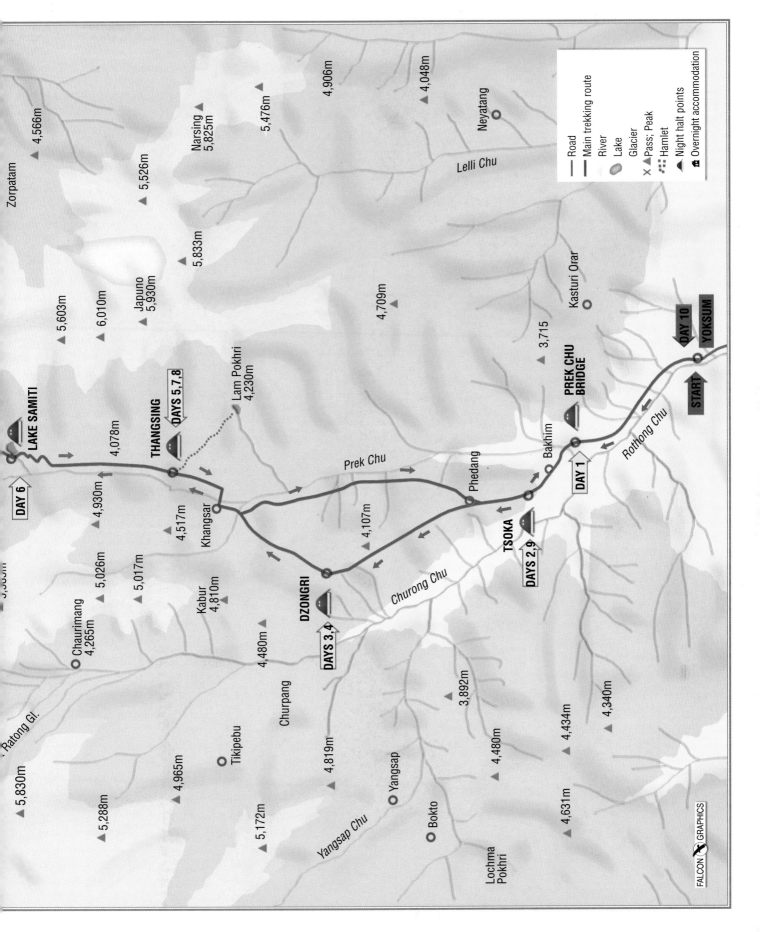

▮I Prek Chu valley leading on to Gocha La

gained 3,000 ft / 915 m on the first day itself, which could be a strain.

▮I **DAY 2**: The first half is hard. You reach the Bakhim hut after a steep climb. Another ninety-minute walk through a thick oak and rhododendron forest brings you to the Tibetan settlement of Tsoka (9,860 ft / 3,005 m). It has a camping site and gives a tantalising glimpse of the conical top of the Pandim Peak. Look out for photo opportunities.

▮I **DAYS 3,4**: Climb steeply through a thick forest till you reach the little meadow at Phedang halfway to Dzongri (13,100 ft / 3,993 m). Witness the transition from the temperate to the alpine zone. As you walk through dense forests on the first three days, the most widespread plant is the cobra head plant. You can also see at least two dozen different varieties of wild roses. Rhododendrons would, of course, be in full bloom in late March or April. The flowers to look out for, however, are the orchids. In April, *Coelogyne ochracea*, a white orchid with orange-red spots on the mid-lobes, grows on the rocks. Columbines, pheasant's eyes, wild strawberries, and primulas are aplenty. June through July sees a wild

flowering of the primulas. Pitch camp next to the tourist hut at Dzongri. Though there is a better site with great views, a twenty-minute walk up on the Dzongri meadow, staying below is a more discrete option. The best time for a walk up the meadow and then beyond to the crest of the ridge is at 5.30 a.m. when the first sunrays hit the mountains. As you soak in the view of the summits of the Kabru Complex, Gocha, Rathong, and the Pandim Peak, from behind them all emerges the Kanchenjunga, shimmering majestically. Back in the camp for breakfast, spend the day sauntering around. Those feeling active can go for

■I Pandim Peak from Dzongri ridge at sunrise

a hike to a side ridge top to get a view of the Rhatong glacier.

■I **DAY 5**: Well into the trek, you are back in the forests after climbing the Dzongri Pass (13,450 ft / 4,100 m) and descending steeply. You meet the Prek Chu river again to cross over to the left bank. On a side stream is the Khangsar hut, great to relax in and have lunch. While crossing over, you would see that all the rocks next to the river are pink because of the lichens growing on them. After a slow, two-hour climb, you reach the wide expanse of the Thangsing meadow.

Hooked to the Himalaya

A GREAT explorer who came to Sikkim was Joseph Dalton Hooker. He had trained in medicine but was influenced more by his father, a professor of botany at Glasgow University, Scotland. When twenty-two, he accompanied James Ross, the Polar explorer, on the famous Antarctica Expedition of 1839-43. With his abilities honed on this hazardous but successful voyage, Hooker came to India in 1848, and went at once to Darjeeling. He remained there for two years, studying its great floral variety. His journals have vivid descriptions not only of the flora, but also of the scenery, the people, and the faith by which they lived. Spending many months above the tree line and climbing to more than 18,000 ft / 5,500 m on many occasions, at a time when few peaks of over 14,000 ft / 4,300 m had even been attempted, he finally wrote *Flora of British India*. It is a monumental work in seven volumes, the introduction being over 260 pages. Hooker describes some 4,000 Sikkimese trees, shrubs, and plants, each individually collected, dissected, and studied. Hooker remains one of the very few explorers who made the mysteries of the Himalaya accessible.

■I *Coelogyne corymbosa*. Over sixty-five orchids are found in Sikkim.

■I The mighty Kanchenjunga

Rhododendrons: Painting the trail red

ONE OF the most memorable motifs on a hike in the Kanchenjunga region in spring is that of blood-red rhododendron flowers blooming on a clump of trees surrounded by a dark green jungle of oaks. Seldom in the Himalaya would you come across such a large variety of these flowers. A research expedition organised by Royal Botanical Garden, Edinburgh, in 1990, collected forty-two different species in the region. Believed to have originated more than 100 million years ago in China, *Rhododendron arboreum*, the ancient, most common but stunningly beautiful flower, is found between 5,000 ft and 11,500 ft / 1,500 m and 3,500 m, the most dispersed range for a species. It occupies a large range of elevations in Sikkim, from 5,000 ft to almost 17,000 ft / 1,500 m to 5,200 m. Growing to a height of almost twenty to twenty-five feet in temperate zones, the rhododendron's size shrinks with increasing altitude. *Rhododendron nivale*, an alpine shrub, grows barely a few inches above the ground. On this route, the flowers start blooming in February at lower elevations, and as the snow melts at higher altitudes, the flowers also start appearing. They can be seen at an altitude of 16,000 ft / 5,000 m even in June. Though the most common colour associated with them is red, the rhododendrons are dressed in maroon, scarlet, crimson, pink, mauve, purple, yellow, cream, and white. A few species like *Rhododendron anthopogon*, *Rhododendron dalhousiae* and *Rhododendron triflarum* also exude an aroma. In Himalayan homes, a few leaves are thrown into the fireplace for their fragrance. All over the Himalaya, as in Sikkim, rhododendron flowers are used to make jams, juices and even a heady wine. But, for the trekker, their greatest value lies in the beautiful and constant company they provide.

■| **DAY 6**: A two-and-a-half-hour climb through meadows and you come to the snout of the imposing Onglaktang Glacier. Forty-five minutes of steep climbing brings you to the serene waters of Lake Samiti (or Sungmoteng Cho). Stark and windswept, the lake is classic high-altitude Himalayan wilderness. At a height of nearly 14,000 ft / 4,267 m, a world of gurgling streams flows behind you. Somewhere on a rocky ledge a snow leopard contemplates the world as prayer flags flutter wildly in the cold, ceaseless wind – a magical and sombre moment to be preserved.

■| **DAY 7**: Early morning, catch the sun hitting the peaks of the Kabru complex and the Gocha Peak, and also get a great view of the Onglaktang Glacier. After a steep five-hour climb, reach the Gocha La at 16,208 ft / 4,940 m, the highest point on this trek, where you nearly touch the Kanchenjunga's regal splendour. Now, it's all the way down to Yoksum, Darjeeling, or wherever you came from.

■| **DAYS 8, 9, 10**: After a day's rest at Thangsing, from where a three-hour walk could take you to Lam Pokhri, take a detour at the Khangsar hut on a narrow trail to Phedang to rejoin the main trail and reach Tsoka in the evening. Porters and yaks, however, have to follow the main route to Dzongri because the trail is too narrow. A brisk seven-hour walk on what is now a familiar trail, and you are back at Yoksum. The trail has ended; the metal road begins.

▮❙ The peak of Ama Dablam that dominates the Everest trail; facing page top: Annapurna South

4

High on Nepal

NEPAL was founded by Ne-Muni, from whom the nation takes its name. In the second half of the first millennium B.C., the Kirantis ruled over Kathmandu valley. Around the same time, Prince Siddhartha Gautama was born in Lumbini, capital of the Lichchavi kingdom of southern Nepal. He became the Buddha. The Lichchavis replaced the Kirantis around 200 A.D. and ruled till the ninth century. Nepal entered its Golden Age under the Malla kings who ruled for more than five hundred years till 1768. But, infighting disintegrated the kingdom. After about two decades, Prithvi Narain Shah, king of the Gorkhas, reunified Nepal and in 1768 took over the reigns. The former king, Birendra Bir Bikram Shah Dev, was a direct descendant of Shah.

In 1846, Jung Bahadur Rana, a young general, conspired with the Queen Regent to eliminate all the top leaders. The queen was banished and the Ranas ruled the country till 1950. In between, the British became major players, with the Ranas conceding territory to imperial India. Nepal's present boundaries were formed then.

To an outsider, oblivious of the intricacies of Nepalese socio-political life, the country remains a paradise of breathtaking landscapes. The presence of the Everest and 26,248 ft / 8,000 m peaks is overwhelming, and almost all legendary names in twentieth-century mountaineering have traversed this region. But Nepal also offers exciting opportunities for trekking, climbing, rafting, and observing wildlife.

It was only in 1949 that Nepal opened its frontiers to foreigners. All early attempts at climbing Everest were made from Tibet on the north face of the peak. The much-discussed 1924 attempt by George Mallory and Andrew Irvine was also on this face. Last seen climbing towards the summit at 27,950 ft / 8,525 m, the two of them disappeared under a cover of clouds …. Success came only in 1953 on the south summit.

The three-year search for a route on the south face of the Everest was a high point of climbing history. All attempts from the Tibet side had failed. An expedition led by an American, Dr Charles Houston entered the Solu Khumbu region, the home of the Sherpas. Bill Tilman, the famous British explorer, was a member of the

▌I Khumbu Glacier from the viewpoint of Kala Pathar

expedition, and he and Houston laid the foundation of a route up the Everest via the West Cwm. (Cwm, a mountaineering term, refers to a bowl of snow surrounded by mountains.)

Next year, in 1951, Eric Shipton, the doyen of pre-war mountaineering, led a crack team of climbers from England and New Zealand to explore the West Cwm and the Khumbu icefall. A young lad called Edmund Hillary joined up with Shipton. His apprenticeship under Shipton was to have a far-reaching effect. Under primitive conditions of transport and communications, the team had to begin walking right from Jogbani, the road head on the Indian border. It took them almost a month to reach Namche Bazaar in Khumbu, braving rain and leech-infested jungles. During the next three weeks the team climbed areas nobody had seen. Very soon they realised the only way up was through the Khumbu icefall, a treacherous arena where death could strike without notice. Squeezed between the steep slopes of Everest's West Ridge and Nuptse, the icefall is prone to avalanches and rigged with crevasses. More people have been killed there than anywhere else on the mountain. The team made two attempts to climb it. On the first, four of them including Shipton and Hillary were almost swept to death in a crevasse. The second put Shipton and Tom Bourdillon on top of the icefall. They looked up the way destiny had reserved for others to tread upon.

On 29 May 1953, Edmund Hillary and Sherpa Sirdar Tenzing Norgay reached the summit of Everest. They also opened up the treasures of the Khumbu region.

Trek I

Ways & Means

Duration
16 days. Beginning from the Lukla airstrip, via Kala Pathar, Cho La and Gokyo Ri, you go back to Namche Bazaar.

Degree of Difficulty
5: Rigorous

Permits
Trekking permits, easily available in Kathmandu, are required for all treks in Nepal.

Getting There
Regular daily flights from Kathmandu to Lukla in small eighteen-seater planes. Make advance bookings as these flights get very full during the trekking season. Alternatively, a seven-hour bus journey from Kathmandu gets you to the road head at Jiri, from where it's a pleasant five-six days of walking to Lukla. The helicopter service from Kathmandu to Syangboche, the airstrip above Namche Bazaar, is irregular.

Best Time
October to early December and mid-March to mid-May. The Cho La could sometimes be under heavy snow and difficult to cross.

Altitude
Acclimatisation is of utmost importance as many days involve climbing over 3,000 ft / 915 m in one day. Lowest altitude at Phakding on second day – 8,600 ft / 2,621 m. Highest altitude at Chukung Ri and Kala Pathar – over 18,000 ft / 5,500 m. Highest campsites at Lobuje and Gokyo lake – over 15,000 ft / 4,500 m.

Highlights
As many as four of the world's eight highest peaks visible from several points. Spectacular views from many high points like Chukung Ri, Kala Pathar, Cho La, and Gokyo Ri. High altitude mountain scenery including glaciers. A culture-rich area with monasteries, especially at Tangboche, and the hospitable Sherpas.

Support Services
Porters and pack animals (yaks and *dzopkyos*) easily available. Many good lodges offer very good food throughout the trip. These lodges do get very basic and fewer as one goes up. Lukla and Namche Bazaar help stock up on food and camping equipment.

Emergency
Relatively easy to call for helicopter rescue, but very expensive. Basic medical facilities are available at Lukla, Namche, Khunde, and at Pheriche where there is a high-altitude medical camp, usually managed by a Western doctor.

∎I The Tibetan Snowcock

Everest Base Camp

Kathmandu is the gateway to the exciting Khumbu region from where the pinnacles of Everest, Lhotse, Annapurna, Machapuchare, and Dhaulagiri have beckoned explorers. Once the haunt of the flower children, the town is today trying desperately to maintain the old image of a Shangri-La.

There are two ways to reach Khumbu from Kathmandu. A day's drive from the capital brings you to Jiri, the road head. But the approach to Khumbu takes almost a week from there. If you have a lot of time and stamina, walk from Jiri and get acclimatised. The flight from Kathmandu to Lukla in the Khumbu area is breathtaking with an unforgettable succession of mountain panoramas. Be sure to get a seat on the left of the plane and far in front. The flight runs parallel to the Great Himalayan Range, starting with Langtang and Jugal Himal and going

∎I Yaks carry the trekking gear

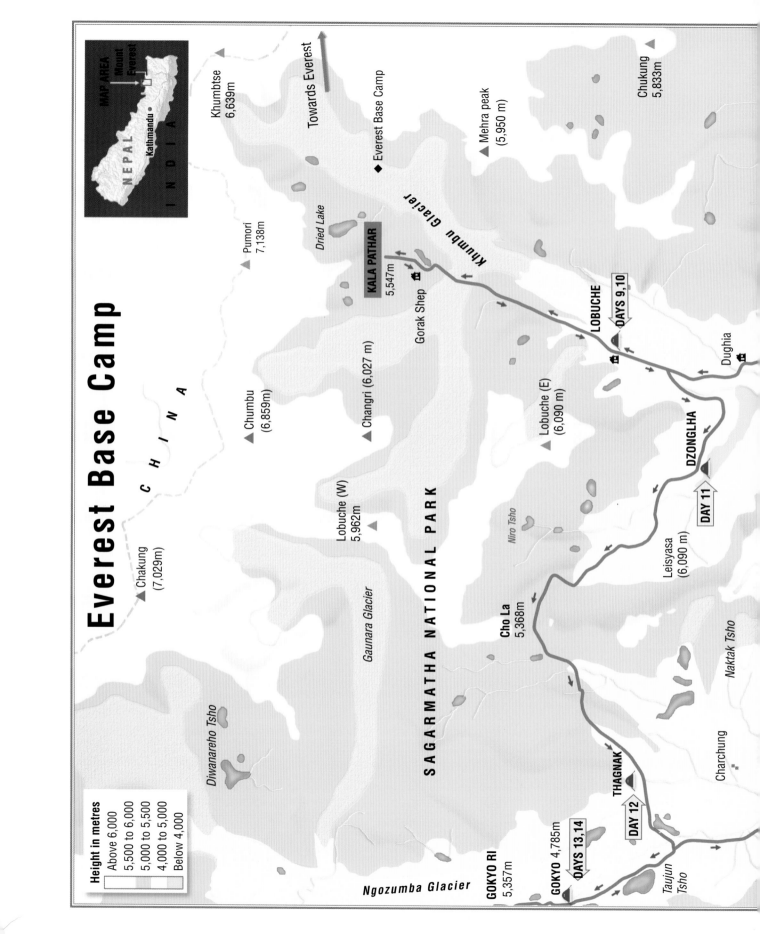

Everest Base Camp

Height in metres
- Above 6,000
- 5,500 to 6,000
- 5,000 to 5,500
- 4,000 to 5,000
- Below 4,000

MAP AREA

Mount Everest

NEPAL

Kathmandu •

INDIA

Chakung (7,029m) ▲

C H I N A

Khumbtse 6,639m ▲

Towards Everest

▲ Pumori 7,138m

Dried Lake

Diwanareho Tsho

▲ Chumbu (6,859m)

◆ Everest Base Camp

Mehra peak (5,950 m) ▲

Chukung 5,833m ▲

KALA PATHAR
5,547m

Gorak Shep

Khumbu Glacier

▲ Changri (6,027 m)

Gaunara Glacier

Lobuche (W) 5,962m ▲

LOBUCHE

DAYS 9,10

Lobuche (E) (6,090 m) ▲

Niro Tsho

DZONGLHA

DAY 11

Dughia

S A G A R M A T H A   N A T I O N A L   P A R K

Leisyasa (6,090 m)

Cho La 5,368m

Maktak Tsho

Charchung

THAGNAK

DAY 12

GOKYO RI 5,357m

GOKYO 4,785m

DAYS 13,14

Ngozumba Glacier

Taujun Tsho

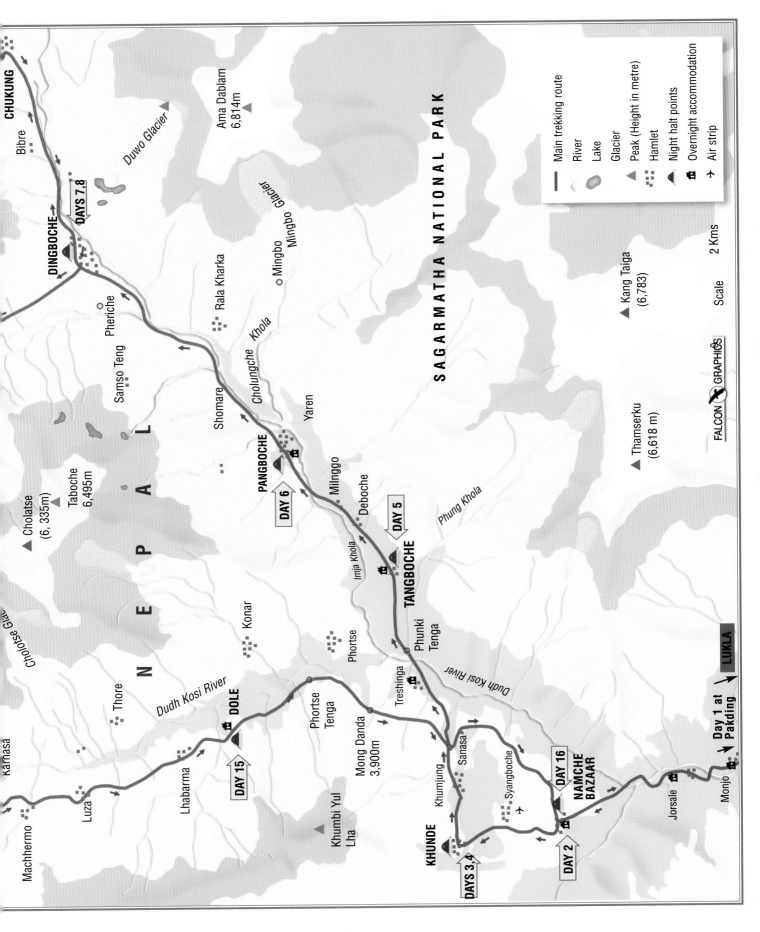

CHUKUNG

Bibre

Ama Dablam
6,814m

Duwo Glacier

DAYS 7,8

DINGBOCHE

Rala Kharka

Mingbo Glacier
Mingbo

Pheriche

Samso Teng

Cholungche Khola

Shomare

Yaren

Cholatse
(6, 335m)

Taboche
6,495m

PANGBOCHE

DAY 6

Milnggo

Deboche

Imja Khola

Phung Khola

DAY 5

TANGBOCHE

Konar

Phortse

Phunki
Tenga

Karnasa

Thore

Dudh Kosi River

DOLE

Phortse
Tenga

Treshinga

Dudh Kosi River

Machhermo

Luza

Lhabarma

Mong Danda
3,900m

DAY 15

Khumjung

Sanasa

Khumbi Yul
Lha

DAYS 3,4

KHUNDE

Syangboche

DAY 16

NAMCHE
BAZAAR

DAY 2

Jorsale

Monjo

Day 1 at
Pakding

LUKLA

S A G A R M A T H A   N A T I O N A L   P A R K

N   E   P   A   L

Cholotse Glac

▲ Kang Taiga
(6,783)

▲ Thamserku
(6,618 m)

Main trekking route

River

Lake

Glacier

▲ Peak (Height in metre)

Hamlet

Night halt points

Overnight accommodation

Air strip

Scale   2 Kms

FALCON GRAPHICS

■I Sunset on Everest, the grand monarch of the Himalaya

on to Cho Oyu and Everest itself. When the plane takes a left into the Dudh Kosi valley, your heart starts pounding at the proximity of the gigantic massifs. You also see a distant piece of land stuck vertically on a mountainside like a stamp on an envelope — the Luki airstrip.

■I **DAY 1**: After reaching Lukla, at 9,000 ft / 2,743 m, walk immediately. This can be tough, but the first day's walk is a gentle descent to the village of Pakding (8,500 ft / 2,590 m), just more than three hours away from the airstrip. After reaching the valley floor, cross a narrow suspension bridge over the Dudh Kosi at Choplung. Make sure that there is no yak or *dzopkyo* (a cross between a yak and a cow) coming from the opposite side — the right of way in the region favours animals! The bridges are sturdy and dependable. The trail to Pakding is a never-ending sequence of tea shops, but the monotony is broken finally when you see tourists guzzling beer at the bars in the village. The day at Pakding should be spent resting.

■I **DAY 2**: You go from Pakding to Namche Bazaar, the fabled headquarters of the Sherpas. Namche was the most vital trading post between Tibet, mainland Nepal and India. With the decline in trade, however, the local economy has depended on the climbing and trekking groups. Every Saturday, a weekly bazaar turns this hamlet into an oriental film set.

The first part of the walk up from Pakding is easy. You enter the Sagarmatha National Park at Monjo early in the day. The Everest region

■l Gyachung Kang (25,990 ft / 7,922 m) at sunset

has been declared a national park and your trekking permit is checked here. This part of the trek has magnificent forests of rhododendrons and magnolias (a large magnolia tree looms near the entrance of the national park). In the nearly four hours of the trek, till the confluence of the rivers Dudh Kosi and Bhote Kosi, you barely climb 900 ft / 275 m. Cross over to the right bank of the Dudh Kosi over a dramatic suspension bridge, then switch back steeply the next 2,000 ft / 610 m to Namche Bazaar. Halfway up is a welcome Chautara (porter's rest stop) from where you get the first view of the Lhotse-Nuptse wall and the tip of Everest.

■l **DAY 3**: Take rest at Namche or go on short walks. One such walk is to the top of the ridge above town, to the national park headquarters. From near this building, a panorama awaits you: Kusum Kanguru, Thamserku, and Kang Taiga on the right; Ama Dablam, the Lhotse-Nuptse wall with Everest showing its crest from behind, and Taboche to your left. Those who feel acclimatised can go to Everest View Hotel, a three-hour walk away, for more views. Be on the look out for the *tahr*, a shaggy goat seen in herds, and the *danphe*, the handsome monal or impeyan pheasant, which is the national bird of Nepal.

■l **DAY 4**: The trail takes you past the Syangboche airfield to Khunde (12,400 ft / 3,780 m), another Sherpa village. This landing strip at 12,200 ft / 3,718 m is used to fly out rather than to fly in because of the acclimatisation problem. The trail is through thick

■l Mount Everest and Khumbu Glacier from Kala Pathar

birch and fir forests. In spring, the rhododendron, the national flower of Nepal, dazzles you. Khunde and Khumjung are twin villages on either side of a stream with Khumbu's sacred mountain, Khumbila, towering above. Edmund Hillary's Himalayan Trust has been active in these villages, running a hospital and a school.

■l **DAY 5**: While going from Khunde to Tangboche monastery, stop at the monastery at Khumjung to look at what is ostensibly a yeti skull! When taken to America for verification in

1960 by Hillary, the scalp was found to be made of antelope skin. The path from Khumjung joins the main trail to Tangboche at Sanasa. It winds its way to Treshinga and then dips steeply to the Phunki Tenga village (10,660 ft / 3,250 m) where you cross over to the other side of the Dudh Kosi. Being the lowest point on the trek, it is also the warmest. Switchbacking up a tough climb, reach Tangboche, the most sacred monastery of the area. Tangboche got burnt in 1989 and was rebuilt by the Sherpas with generous external funds.

■l **DAY 6**: After descending from the ridge, it is a three-hour walk to Pangboche (12,800 ft / 3,900 m). Pitch your camp above the trail for a view of Ama Dablam. A side trail from there takes you to a *yersa* (a high altitude shepherd camp) at Mingbo, spectacularly situated in a valley between Thamserku and Ama Dablam. This is where the base camp is set up for climbing Ama Dablam.

■l **DAYS 7-8**: A simple climb brings you to Dingboche. Just lounge around there, or take a walk. The next two

■I Crossing the Cho La, 17,612 ft / 5,368 m
■I Right: Camp at Dingboche

days are tough. Climb up to the tea shops at Chukung, then to the Chukung Ridge at 17,700 ft / 5,395 m, on a steep trail after crossing the Imja Khola river. Makalu, Imjatse (also called Island Peak), and Baruntse peaks are to your east. In the north, you are just under the Nuptse-Lhotse wall. With the cold night approaching, descend fast to Dingboche.

■I **DAYS 9-10**: On way to Lobuche, you are on the Khumbu glacier and get the first taste of walking on a

lateral moraine. A retreating glacier leaves rocks and stones behind: walking can be taxing on your calves. Take your time and do it in six hours.

The ascent to the Kala Pathar or the Black Peak (18,200 ft / 5,547 m) is your rendezvous with climbing history. From this ridge top in 1951, Shipton and Hillary got a glimpse of a route over the Khumbu icefall. From Lobuche, walk on the moraine for two hours to reach Gorak Shep. From there, start your climb up the Kala Pathar. As you go up, Everest reveals itself a bit and framed by Khumbuse and Nuptse, finally unmasks itself completely. You are standing below Pumori, another giant, surveying the panorama. But the cold wind makes you descend.

■❙ **DAY 11**: Reach the yak herders' summer camp at Dzonglha. The camp is pitched beneath the north wall of Cholatse with the magnificent Thamserku beckoning from the valley.

■❙ The Himalayan Tahr

■❙ The weekly Saturday market at Namche Bazaar

■❙ **DAY 12**: The climb up the Cho La is over a flat field but turns quite steep. In fact, for a short stretch you would be doing four-point climbing! Another steep ascent would bring you to the top of Cho La (17,612 ft / 5,368 m). A sharp descent on the other side would lead to the scree on the Nima Gawa glacier. After crossing the glacier and climbing a ridge for half an hour, you go down to Thagnak (15,300 ft / 4,663 m), another summer camp.

■❙ **DAY 13**: Descend to the Ngozumba glacier flowing from the base of the Cho Oyu and Gyachung Kang. Walk on the glacier for two kilometres (two hours) and then for another two hours on its lateral moraine, climbing up to Gokyo (15,700 ft / 4,785 m). Pitch your camp on the shores of the Dudh Pokhri lake which is covered with ice in spring.

■❙ **DAYS 14-15**: The most enchanting view still awaits the climber at the Gokyo Ri (17,576 ft / 5,357 m) above Dudh Pokhri: four of the fourteen peaks above 26,248 ft / 8,000 m – Everest, Cho Oyu, Lhotse, and Makalu – and huge glaciers tumbling down into valleys, spires, and jagged precipices. This is the wildest arena on earth – nature in its most savage incarnation, yet serene and sombre. Descend from this grand theatre to the moraine, and in seven hours reach the lush forests around Dole meadow.

■❙ **DAY 16**: Back at Namche. After two weeks of isolation, it looks like a metropolis. It's worth your while soaking in the charms of Khumbu for another day.

Trek II

Annapurna Sanctuary

Ways & Means

Around 200,000 years ago, two of Nepal's prominent valleys, Kathmandu and Pokhara, were under water. The Kathmandu valley shows no obvious trace of this. But in and around Pokhara, the take-off point for the Annapurna region, lakes point to the geological past. In Nepali, 'Pokhara' itself refers to a pond. Spread out around the picturesque Phewa lake, the town is a laid-back haven. North of it opens out the panorama of the Annapurna Himal with Machapuchare rising like a sentinel.

Annapurna (the Goddess of Abundance) has beckoned explorers since the time Nepal opened its frontiers in 1949. In fact, Annapurna I was the first 26,248 ft / 8,000 m peak to be climbed when a French expedition led by Maurice Herzog reached the summit in 1950. There are various approaches to the Annapurna Sanctuary Trek. Ours came into prominence when former American President Jimmy Carter wanted to spend time away from his busy schedule on a trip to Nepal, in the late '70s/early '80s. With his need for privacy, a new and short trek with great views was designed. It forms an attractive approach to the main hike to the Sanctuary.

▌ DAY 1: A forty-five-minute drive going to the south west of Pokhara (2,800 ft / 853 m), on the Bhairawa road leads to the Thale Khola stream, often dry in spring. Having climbed

barely 400 ft on the road, begin the trek at a comfortable 3,200 ft / 975 m. Camp the first evening above Bhumdi (5,300 ft / 1,615 m). You get the prized view of Dhaulagiri, visible only during the first three days of the trek.

▌ DAY 2: A dream walk through a dense deciduous forest. There is a profusion of flowers and plant life. It's an ideal place for bird-watching. In the evening, camp in a clearing in a rhododendron forest, a five-minute walk above the trail. The water source is below the campsite on the south side of the mountain.

▌ DAY 3: Immediately after traversing the mountainside, the trail reaches a saddle where many trails join it. After a steep switchbacking trail through thick vegetation, you reach the top of Panchase Lekh and a great view. Coming down from the saddle, then a long traverse and a descent, and you reach a campsite in a grassy area above Badaure village.

▌ DAY 4: The trail meets the conventional entry point to the Sanctuary trek. Leaving the camp, ascend a short while and then go through a long traverse of the mountain on a well-used trail. Finally, descend to Lumle on the Pokhara-Baglung road. After crossing the road, a steady climb of half an hour brings you to Chandarkot village where you enter the Modi Khola valley. Another well laid-out trail through some pretty

Duration
15 days

Degree of Difficulty
4: Moderate to rigorous

Permits
Trekking permits available in Kathmandu, are required for all treks in Nepal.

Getting There
Regular flights to Pokhara from Kathmandu, or a six-hour bus drive. From Pokhara, forty-five minutes by car to the road head.

Best Time
October to mid-December and mid-March to mid-May.

Altitude
Trek starts at only 3,200 ft / 975 m; highest campsite is at Machapuchare base camp, 12,200 ft / 3,718 m.

Highlights
Spectacular views at President's camp on Day 2 and from the Austrian camp on the last day; thick bamboo, pine, and rhododendron forests in the upper reaches; hot water sulphur spring on the Modi Khola; excellent bird-watching opportunities.

Support Services
Porters available in Pokhara where they must be pre-arranged. Good lodges and food available throughout except for the first three days. Or, start the trek from Lumle village and miss out on the first three days.

Emergency
Ghandrung is a major government base with basic medical and rescue services. A rescue helicopter can be called for even from the base camp at Machapuchare, but is expensive.

Annapurna Sanctuary

MAP AREA

C H I N A

N E P A L

●Kathmandu

I N D I A

N E P A L

Tilicho Lake

5,367m

6,170m

Tarke Kang 7,069m

Gaudharba Chuli 6,248m

MACHAPUCHARE BASE CAMP 3,720m

Machapuchare

Mardi Himal 5,587m

5,672m

Khangsha Kang 7,485m

7,202m

Singu Chuli ▲ 6,499m

Tharpu Chuli

5,663m

DAYS 9-10

ANNAPURNA BASE CAMP 4,095m

Hinku

DAYS 11-12

4,130m

Tilicho Peak 7,134m

6,648m

6,364m

Annapurna I 8,091m

Hiunchuli 6,441m

DAY 8 DHOBAN

5,675m

Barah shikhar 7,647m

6,721m

7,219m Annapurna South

4,941m

Sauru ▲3,803m

North 7,061m Nilgiri Central 6,904m

▲ Nilgiri South 6,765m 6,839m

4,088m

4,185m

4,511m

5,349m

4,140m

4,703m

4,267m

Kalku river

Upalla Lete Lete Kalopani

Nimek 3,904m

Pangbu

Tongdung

Mirisiti khola

4,752

3,493m

3,592m

3,730m

4,112m

khola

Pangdor

3,704m

Ghasa

Talbagar 3,421m

Kabre

Bhalobas

Titre Dana Garpan

Bhatu Khola

Tatopani

Ghara

Dhoba

Relative heights in metres

Above 5,000
3,000-5,000
1,000-3,000
Below 1,000

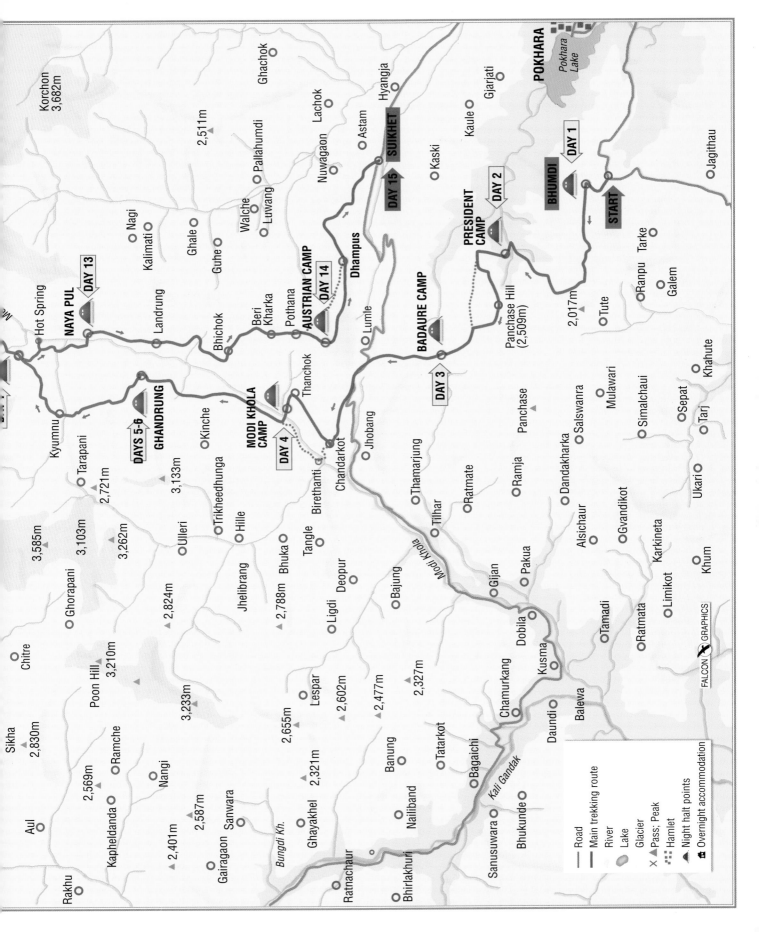

■I Annapurna South and Annapurna I

fields in spring and you reach the campsite (4,900 ft / 1,493 m) on the river bank, short of Bhichul village.

■I **DAYS 5-6**: The route crosses over to the right bank to meet a trail coming up from Birethanti village. It also serves as an approach to the Annapurna Sanctuary trek. Winding your way through buckwheat fields in spring, around busy little Gurung villages, you reach the prosperous village of Ghandrung high above the Modi Khola. These are hallowed grounds of the Gurung warriors, one

of the proud races that make up the Gorkha regiments. It's not at all surprising to see a Victoria Cross hanging gingerly next to a window!

After five tiring days, take a well-deserved rest on the sixth. Visit the Annapurna Conservation Area Project Headquarters at Ghandrung (6,400 ft / 1,950 m).

■I **DAY 7**: Leave Ghandrung to reach the small Kyumnu Danda pass (7,400 ft / 2,255 m). It's great for a brief stop-over with sheer drops on both sides and a great mountain view.

Now, descending to the Kyumnu Khola, go past lodges and tea shops to the river bank to cross over to the other side. Climbing up a steep gradient to the top of the ridge, you traverse the hillside to descend gently towards Chomrong, the last permanent settlement in the valley. Chomrong forms a natural entrance to the Annapurna Sanctuary. From there, you get a prominent view of Machapuchare.

■I **DAY 8**: The trail enters the Sanctuary proper. Closer to the

■I Machapuchare or the Fish Tail peak, considered sacred by the locals

Annapurna wall, the sheer expanses of ice, rock, and snow and the quirky way in which sudden blizzards start blowing are mesmerising. Chris Bonnington, the mountaineering legend of our times, led a British expedition up the south face of Annapurna in 1970. This was often regarded as the first great technical climb in the Himalaya, and since then the Sanctuary has become a sacred centre for hikers. Descending into the Chomrong Khola valley, crossing over to the other side on a metal bridge, and then climbing steeply for half an hour, you reach Sinuwa. There, you enter a dense oak and rhododendron forest. The trail goes past the small settlement of Kuldi Ghar and descends to Bamboo Lodge, a collection of hotels in a clearing. But the forest is wet and humid and infested with insects, so be careful. The trail ascends continuously up the side of the canyon (despite some descents to cross streams) to reach Dhoban. Now you can camp only next to the lodges, according to the Sanctuary's rules.

■I **DAY 9**: The trail climbs through a thick bamboo forest to reach the pastures of Tomo above the timberline. There you get the first views of the Gangpurna and Annapurna III peaks. A little ahead is Panchenin Barha, the narrowest point in the canyon marked by a trail-side shrine. Prior to 1956, 'impurities' such as pork, beef, chicken, garlic, eggs, foreigners, and low caste people, were not allowed to go beyond this point. But times have changed. The valley opens up from here and a steep climb brings you to the Hinku cave, often

■I Left to right: A panoramic view of Annapurna South, Annapurna I, Hiunchuli, Machapuchare, Annapurna IV and II

used as a shelter. The trail descends to cross a small stream at Deorali. The area is prone to avalanches and landslides because of the sheer heights on both the sides. Depending on the previous year's avalanches, the trail crosses the Modi Khola or stays on this side. At Bagar, rejoin the trail if you have crossed over. Thereafter the climb is tough. Walking over the scree, ascend steeply to cross a wooden bridge over a small stream to reach the Machapuchare Base Camp at 12,207 ft / 3,720 m. This is a nine-hour walk and it's best to begin early. The views are breathtaking.

■I **DAY 10**: Stay at the Machapuchare Base Camp the following day as you can walk up to the Annapurna Base Camp in two hours and be back by the evening. Leaving early, you walk westward up between the moraine of the Annapurna South glacier and Hiunchuli. Then going up a moraine ridge you go past a few lodges to reach the Annapurna Base Camp. Try to be there early to spend at least three hours in clear weather. By afternoon, the clouds will restrict your view. The panorama there is stupendous – on your east is the west face of Machapuchare which turns crimson with the setting sun (a treat worth waiting for); the north-east is dominated by Annapurna III and Gangpurna, and up ahead is Tent Peak. The gigantic wall of Annapurna I is on the north-west, and the south-west is adorned by Annapurna South and Hiunchuli. Those who have technical experience, rations, and

■I Right: The view from Panchase Lekh

good climbing gear could attempt Tent Peak (18,580 ft / 5,663 m) for even better views.

■I **DAYS 11-12**: Go back to Dhoban or Bamboo camp via the route you came up. On Day 12, return to Chomrong.

■I **DAY 13**: Take a half-hour detour beyond the village by going down the stone steps to the Modi Khola river. Just short of where the trail levels out, there is a diversion to hot water springs near the river bank. A dip in

■I An avalanche down the face of Annapurna I; below: Special bamboo swings put up during the spring

the sulphur water can be therapeutic. After a stopover, climb up the main trail and reach the Kyumnu Khola river. Crossing over and walking another half hour, you reach the Naya Pul (the new bridge), a collection of hotels and tea houses next to a suspension bridge over the Modi Khola. The campsite is on the other side of the bridge.

■I **DAY 14**: The penultimate day on the trek is eight hours long, so it's advisable to start early. In an hour and a half, you reach Landrung village. A walk of three hours followed by an hour's steep climb brings you to the Beri Kharka pass. After descending to Pothana village, leave the main trail to climb through a thick rhododendron forest onto a ridge top descending from Machapuchare. A walk through grassy meadows leads to the campsite, the Austrian camp, used by mountaineers from that country in the '60s.

■I **DAY 15**: Join the main trail at Dhampus to descend to the road head at Suikhet on the Baglung-Pokhara road. A forty-minute drive brings you back to Pokhara.

Trek III

Around Annapurna

Ways & Means

The topographical range you cover, the different climatic zones you encounter, the bewildering variety of plant and animal life you observe, and the fascinating cultures and people you meet make this trek nothing less than a revelation. The trail that follows the Marsyandi river up towards the Thorang La is rich in history.

■ **DAY 1**: There are two main approaches to the points from which one can embark upon the trek. You could fly from Kathmandu to Pokhara and then drive two and a half hours to reach the road head, or you could drive straight from Kathmandu to Dumre and then follow the Marsyandi up to Phalasangu (2,000 ft / 610 m), from where you could start walking. The drive would take around five

hours. Conventionally trekkers drive up to Besi Sahar further up the Marsyandi valley before beginning their hike, but considering it is a dreary town hit by construction mania, Phalasangu provides a saner starting point. After the uneventful drive, walk across a wooden bridge to the left bank of the Marsyandi to reach the campsite on a fallow field after a fifteen-minute hike.

■ **DAY 2**: Being used to the hype about the towering heights of the Nepalese mountains, it's a welcome surprise to walk through the Himalayan foothills. Teeming with insect life, the trail goes past villages and rice fields, crossing side streams with coloured butterflies and huge spider webs. Having climbed 500 ft after an easy five-hour walk, you

Duration
15 days

Degree of Difficulty
4: Moderate to rigorous

Permits
Available at Kathmandu.

Getting There
The drive to the road head at Phalasangu is equidistant from Kathmandu and Pokhara. Leave the highway at Dumre and follow the Marsyindi valley to the road head.

Best Time
October to mid-December and mid-March to mid-May. Thorang La could be under heavy snow cover by early December and in March.

Altitude
The range of altitude varies greatly, from 2,000 ft / 610 m at Phalasangu (the road head) to 17,700 ft / 5,395 m on the Thorang La.

Highlights
Spectacular views of the Annapurna massif from the upper Marsyandi valley; Braga *gompa* and Muktinath temple.

Support Services
Porters easily available at the road head at Phalasangu; food and basic guest houses available throughout.

Emergency
A helicopter rescue can be called for from many places. There is an airstrip at Hongde (near Manang) with irregular flights from Kathmandu and Pokhara. Only basic medical facilities are available at Manang.

■I Annapurna III from the lake high above Braga village

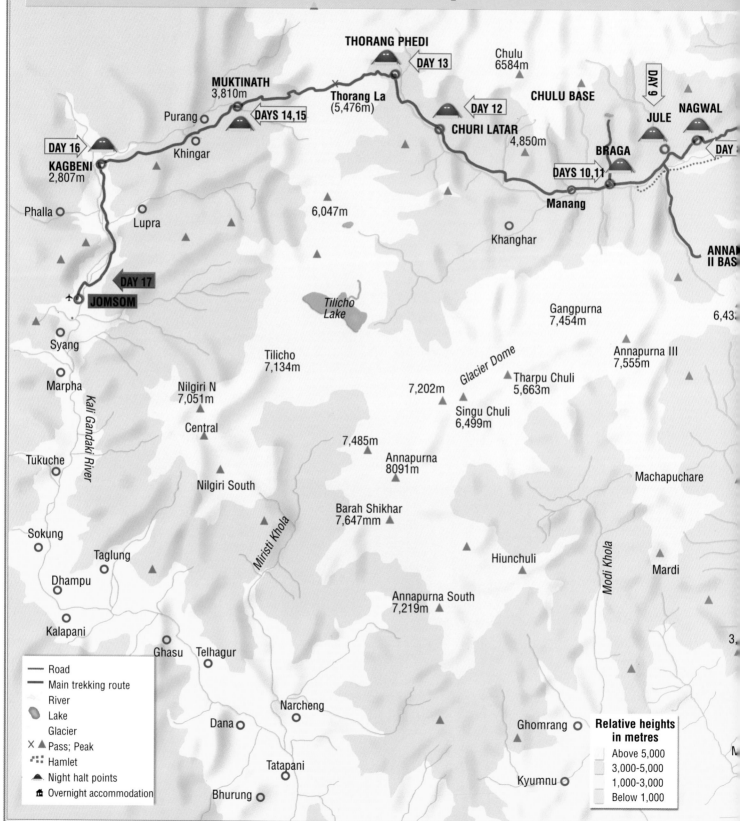

Around Annapurna

THORANG PHEDI
DAY 13

Chulu
6584m

MUKTINATH
3,810m

Thorang La
(5,476m)

DAY 9

CHULU BASE

NAGWAL

JULE

Purang

DAYS 14,15

DAY 12

CHURI LATAR
4,850m

DAY

DAY 16

Khingar

BRAGA

KAGBENI
2,807m

DAYS 10,11

Phalla

Lupra

Manang

6,047m

DAY 17

Khanghar

JOMSOM

ANNA
II BAS

Syang

Tilicho
Lake

Gangpurna
7,454m

6,43

Marpha

Tilicho
7,134m

Glacier Dome

Tharpu Chuli
5,663m

Annapurna III
7,555m

Nilgiri N
7,051m

7,202m

Central

Singu Chuli
6,499m

Machapuchare

7,485m

Nilgiri South

Annapurna
8091m

Tukuche

Barah Shikhar
7,647mm

Modi Khola

Mardi

Sokung

Hiunchuli

Taglung

Dhampu

Annapurna South
7,219m

Kalapani

3

Ghasu
Telhagur

Ghomrang

Kyumnu

Narcheng

Dana

**Relative heights
in metres**

Above 5,000

Tatapani

3,000-5,000

1,000-3,000

Bhurung

Kyumnu

Below 1,000

Kali Gandaki River

Miristi Khola

— Road
— Main trekking route
~ River
◗ Lake
Glacier
✕ ▲ Pass; Peak
∴ Hamlet
⛺ Night halt points
🏠 Overnight accommodation

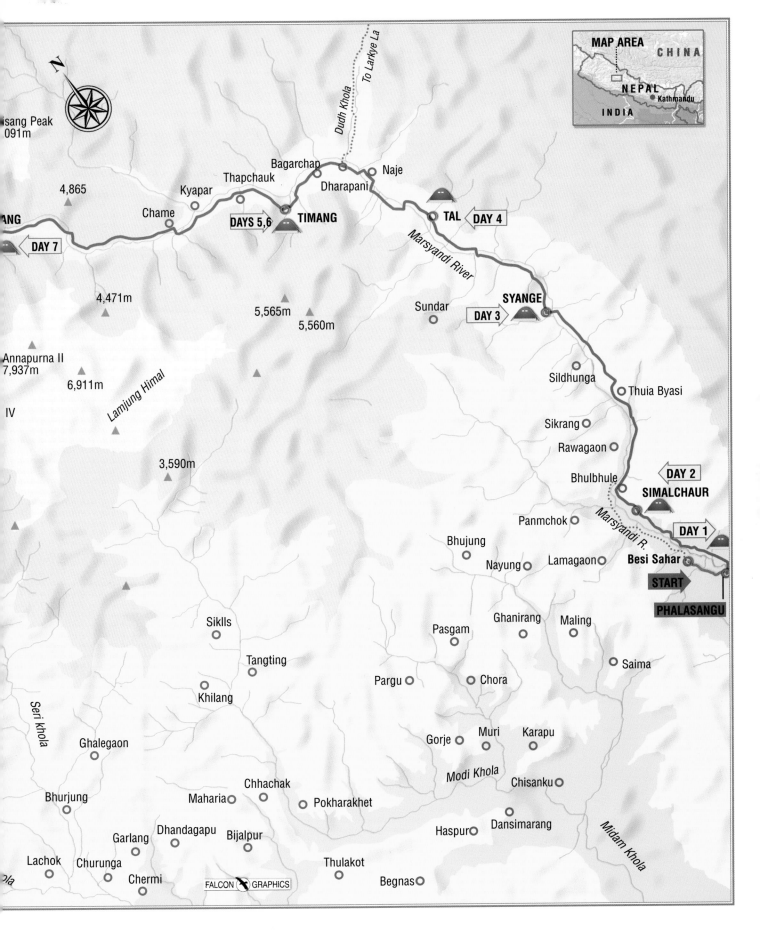

reach the village of Simal Chaur (2,500 ft / 762 m) in the afternoon.

■I **DAY 3**: Within an hour, you reach the village of Bhulbhule on a bend in the Marsyandi. As the river turns eastwards, the main trail from Besi Sahar crosses over to the left bank. Here, at the bend you get lovely views of Manaslu, Himalchuli, and Ngadi Chuli (also known as Manaslu II and earlier known as Peak 29). Carrying on upstream, a switchbacking climb takes you to Bahundanda (or Brahmin Hill) at 4,300 ft / 1,311 m. Descending to the river bank, reach the beach camp at Syange. It is in the middle of a large cultivated valley and marks the end of rice cultivation in this area. This, in effect, points to the beginning of a drier climate.

■I **DAY 4**: The Marsyandi valley narrows down beyond Syange as the river enters a gorge. Switching over briefly to the right bank and then to the left at Chamche, the trail has been blasted out of the wall of the canyon. The old trail, on which the salt trade moved, climbed up and down the cliffs on bamboo ladders high above the river. It can still be seen occasionally where it crosses the face of the high cliffs.

Snaking past the villages of Jagat and Chamche within the canyon, the trail descends briefly as the valley suddenly opens into a large plateau. After a gradual climb you reach the campsite of Tal (5,400 ft / 1,646 m) on a green

■I Early morning at the village of Pisang (10,200 ft / 3,109 m)

█I Annapurna III and Gangpurna peak (to the extreme right)

meadow. A waterfall, called Tal, descending from the Ngadi Chuli Peak adds to the charm. Tal (Lake in Nepalese) was created a few hundred years ago when the Marsyandi gorge was blocked by a landslide. The lake filled in with debris from the mountains and became a flat valley. Tal is also the gateway to the predominantly Buddhist district of Manang.

■ **DAY 5**: Leaving Tal, the ascent continues on the eastern bank. The trail is cut out of rock walls. As the valley broadens out, you reach the confluence of Marsyandi and Dudh Khola at Dharapani. Dudh Khola descends from the Larkya La, one of the passes that lead into Tibet. At Dharapani, trekking permits are checked. A short distance away is Thonje village that leads to the Larkya La. Crossing over to the left bank at Thonje, where the river bends westwards, the trail climbs steadily through a pine forest to reach Bagarchap, a Tibetan-looking village with a monastery. Leaving the main trail, climb steeply for forty-five minutes to an hour to reach a pretty meadow at Timang (8,500 ft / 2,591 m).

■ **DAY 6**: Keeping camp at Timang, look for the lost trail to Namun Bhanjyang. The old salt trade trail passed over this difficult pass to reach the upper Marsyandi valley because the path up the gorge was dangerous. As it often happens, the creation of a new route has obliterated the old path from collective memory. So, take someone familiar with the old route.

It's a rewarding day's walk up the high altitude pastoral setting with hundreds of grazing sheep, goats, and water buffaloes.

■ **DAY 7**: Climbing westward through a lush forest, you reach the village of Thapchauk (9,400 ft / 2,865 m). The trail descends to Kyapar, near the confluence of the Marsyandi and Nar. Situated in a meadow, Kyapar is the entry point to the mysterious Nar valley, which is prohibited to foreigners. With a population of barely a thousand people and a culture different from Manang, Nar valley remains an enigma. A short walk away is Chame (8,700 ft / 2,652 m), the headquarters of Manang district. Till 1973, Chame marked the end of the trail in the Manang district as trekkers were not allowed to go beyond it. Now, of course, trekkers prefer to move on as it gets extremely cold here in winter and summer. The trail climbs to Pisang (10,200 ft / 3,109 m) from Chame and goes in and out of the forest, skirting the walled apple orchards of Bhratang. The highest inhabited village in the Gyasumdo valley, Bhratang, was once a camp for the Khampa fighters who controlled the nearby Marsyandi bridge. Approaching this bridge, you see the dramatic Paungda Danda rock face, an imposing cliff of granite rising to more than 5,000 ft / 1,500 m from the river. Soon the panorama of the twenty-five-kilometre long upper Marsyandi valley opens up as you climb over a ridge marked with fluttering prayer flags. The two-part village of Pisang lies just ahead.

■| Braga Gompa

■ **DAY 8**: Leave the main trail to Manang and climb up to upper Pisang after crossing the Marsyandi river on your way to Gvaru and Nagwal. A steep zigzag climb brings you to Gvaru (12,000 ft / 3,657 m) from where you get spectacular views of Annapurna II, III, and IV mountains, the Gangpurna glacier dome, and the Lamjung Himal peaks. Just outside Gvaru is Tiwol Danda, a red fort which is on a cliff, built by the Raja of Manang. A forty-five-minute walk brings you to Nagwal and to views of the Great Barrier above the hidden Tilicho lake to the west. Camp at Nagwal (12,000 ft / 3,657 m) just outside the village.

■ **DAY 9**: Descend to the valley floor and cross the Marsyandi and the main trail to climb up the ridge line leading to the Annapurna III massif for great views. Return to the valley floor; cross the river and walk through a thick forest to camp in a large clearing near Jule village.

■ **DAY 10**: Descend to the river to join the main trail that has crossed over to the left bank. It's an easy walk and there are lovely views of Annapurna III and Gangpurna. The trail reaches the cliff-side perch of Braga. Tucked under high sandstone cliffs, Braga (Place of the White Cliff) is a Tibetan village with 200 houses, all balanced precariously atop one another. The craggy cliffs form a natural amphitheatre around the meadow below. The monastery there is the largest in the district. Manang village is just a half-hour walk from Braga but people prefer to camp at Braga to avoid the crowds at Manang. You could also retrace your steps on the high trail to Ser Gompa, a short walk away.

■ **DAY 11**: Explore the side valley next to Braga. Climb a steep switchbacking trail of almost 3,000 ft / 900 m and another tough climb of thirty to forty-five minutes to reach a lake surrounded by towering peaks. Chulu East and Chulu West and the glacier of the Pisang peak are reflected in the waters. Across the valley, you can see Annapurna I and III, Gangpurna and the magnificent Tilicho Peak. Wild flowers bloom all over the magnificent vistas. This is a

■I Braga village and the campsite way below

most rewarding day for an exploratory walk. Then, you descend all the way back to camp at Braga.

■I **DAY 12**: The trail reaches Manang village within an hour, staying on the left bank. This is the largest village in upper Marsyandi valley or Nyeshang. Dramatically situated next to the huge icefall that descends from the north face of Gangpurna with a sombre-looking glacial lake at its foot, Manang, despite its trade fixation, is a charming place. With a glorious view of Lamjung, Annapurna II, III, and IV, and Gangpurna, the village is an ideal spot for a brief halt. Going past Manang, you soon reach the confluence of the Khanghar and Jhorgeng Kholas that join to make the Marsyandi river. The path up the Khanghar Kholas goes to the Tilicho Lake and the peak. Crossing the nearby Meso Kanta pass, one can reach the Kali Gandaki valley. But our trail goes up the Jhorgeng Khola and a short steep climb brings you to

■I A bridge over the fast-flowing Marsyandi

the Churi Latar camp (13,700 ft / 4,176 m) that can get quite cold at night.

■I **DAY 13**: The valley narrows down after the Churi Latar camp. A slow uphill climb, which is part of an unstable scree slope, brings you to Thorang Phedi (14,450 ft / 4,404 m) or The Foot of the Thorang. The countryside around is the typical habitation of the snow leopard and its prey, such as the blue sheep. Sighting the snow leopard, however, requires a penance.

■I **DAY 14**: Follow the trail over the Thorang La (17,700 ft / 5,476 m). A pass of this height is not to be trifled with and you should cross it only if you are fit and at ease with the height and the intense cold. Any discomfort at Thorang Phedi and you should head back to Manang. Also, no attempt should be made to cross the pass in bad weather as one can get lost. Immediately after leaving Thorang Phedi, the trail climbs on to the steepest section. The trail goes over many a false summit. Traversing a few canyons by moraine, it reaches

the top of this moonscape country. The twin peaks of Yakawa Kang and Khatung Kang flank the pass (both over 21,000 ft / 6,400 m). Looking south, get your last glimpse of the Annapurnas. The Dhaulagiri Himal is on the west and to the north, Mustang beckons. You are 2,000 ft / 600 m above Mont Blanc. But don't spend too much time on the top: sharp winds blow. The descent is not steep at first. Two hours down you get a great view of Dhaulagiri (26,795 ft / 8,167 m) and the Tukuche peaks till you reach the temples of Muktinath.

■ **DAY 15**: The next most holy place after Pashupatinath for the Hindus of Nepal, Muktinath is famous for the Jwala Mai Temple. There a blue flame of natural gas is accompanied by a trickle of water. Easily explained in terms of a chemical reaction, for the believer it remains a clear case of a divine phenomenon. Brahma, the Creator, is supposed to have made an offering there. The day after crossing the Thorang La should be spent resting or visiting a monastery on the other side of Jhang Khola in Chengar village.

■ **DAY 16**: You can reach Jomson on the same day on a higher trail or by taking the longer route via Kagbeni (9,100 ft / 2,774 m). On the crossroads to Dolpo, Mustang, and Manang, Kagbeni is a little place caught in a time warp. With its crumbling mud houses, narrow dark alleys, ruins of an old fort and a red-walled monastery, it looks like the set of a period film. The trail stays high above the stream from Muktinath and goes past the Jharkot fortress to descend and reach the pebbled bank of the Kali Gandaki, leading to

Kagbeni. This part of the Gandaki valley is known for its fossils.

■ **DAY 17**: The last day is a dusty walk through the Kali Gandaki valley. Try reaching Jomsom before 11 a.m. because that's when the wind gains momentum. Do not camp in the open. From Jomsom, continue the walk for another week down the Pokhara valley or take the highly recommended flight to the same place. A day later, your flight swoops past unbelievable vistas through this deep gorge – a thrilling end to a delightful trek.

....

Trek IV

Magical Mustang

Situated far from everywhere on the north-eastern border of Nepal with Tibet, the fabled kingdom of Mustang is a classic example of oriental mystique slipping ever so schemingly into the enticing embrace of the modern market economy. Create seductive hype, ensure restricted entry, keep the price close to the surrounding peaks, and then load the booty on to the nearest Sherpa and let the cash register jingle merrily all the way to Kathmandu. The fact that people would beg, borrow, steal, bribe, kill, or die to reach Mustang testified to the success of the brand management exercise that preceded and followed the opening of this area in 1991. But how and why did this happen?

The intrigue and drama that followed immediately after China's annexation of Tibet in the late '50s

was, in a way, responsible for Mustang's mystification. Being close to the border, it became a centre for guerilla operations against the Chinese. Khampa soldiers, a Tibetan warrior tribe, waged a war against the Red Guards. But Nepal soon disarmed the rebels.

However, the secrecy associated with Mustang continued for almost two decades more as negotiations regarding the border took a long time. Meanwhile, Tibet had become out of bounds. Given the fact that Mustang had the same cobalt blue sky, similar barren mountains, and fostered the grand hope of Nirvana, eager glances were flashed in its direction. Nepal needed a little Tibet of its own. Mustang was it.

Today, Mustang is accessible – at a price. His Majesty's Government takes a permit fee of $70 per day and

double that for the mandatory liaison officer who goes with a trekking group. You are not allowed to venture out alone. There is a limit on the permits issued per year. So, Mustang is for an exclusive club of those who can pay. But environmental sanity requires less elitist solutions. Over the last couple of years, however, with fewer people willing to fork out the high price, traffic to Mustang has reduced to a trickle.

Tucked behind the Annapurna and Dhaulagiri massifs, Mustang forms the watershed of the Kali Gandaki that cuts through the Great Himalayan Range to shape the deepest gorge in the world. Carrying a huge volume of glacial waters, it contributes to the enormous demand for water in the Gangetic basin. Geographically, thus, it is one of the most important areas of the Himalayan system. Legend has it

Ways & Means

Duration
13 days

Degree of Difficulty
4: Moderate to rigorous

Permits
All trekking in Nepal requires a fee, either in Kathmandu or, in this case, at Kagbeni. It is US $ 700 for ten days and $ 70 per day thereafter. Indians are not required to pay the charge.

Getting There
The trek begins and ends at Jomsom, deep in the Kali Gandaki valley. No roads mean one can fly in or walk up the valley in five to seven days. There are flights from Pokhara in eighteen-seater aircraft that must be booked. Pokhara is connected by road and flight from Kathmandu.

Best Time
October to mid-December and mid-March to mid-May.

Altitude
Jomsom, the starting point is at 9,000 ft / 2,745 m and the highest point is on top, of a small pass at 13,800 ft / 4,206 m, just before reaching the town of Lo-Manthang, which is the highest campsite at 12,125 ft / 3,695 m.

Highlights
The cultural richness, especially of the interesting fortified town of Lo-Manthang; spectacular Buddhist monasteries and villages perched on hillsides. The bleakness and aridness lend beautiful brown and red hues to the mountains, best brought out in the spectacular sunsets.

Support Services
Reasonable guest houses and tea shops all along the trail. Jomsom and Lo-Manthang also provide basic food provisions. Some camping equipment can be bought at Jomsom and Kagbeni, but it must be brought along from Pokhara. Porters and horses can be quite easily hired from Jomsom at short notice.

Emergency
Basic medical facilities are available in Jomsom. However, it is possible to communicate from Lo-Manthang and call for a helicopter rescue, though that is very expensive.

that Guru Padmasambhava once killed and disembowelled an ogress troubling Mustang's denizens. It is believed that it was her blood that turned the hills red and her putrid liver that gave them their blue streaks.

▮▮ **DAY 1**: Fly from Pokhara to Jomsom (8,957 ft / 2,730 m), the administrative capital of Mustang. Rushing through the Kali Gandaki gorge, the planes seem puny under the looming Annapurna and Dhaulagiri. The landscape is stark and naked – as harsh as truth itself. Only the green fields put up a sylvan pretence. Jomsom is the usual airstrip, police post, army camp town. After crossing the wooden bridge to the river's east bank, the trail can follow the river bed or move higher on the east bank, depending on the season and the river flow. The trail reaches Kagbeni (9,055 ft / 2,760 m) at the confluence of the Kali Gandaki and Jhong Khola. An old fort in ruins and a red Sakyapa monastery dominate the village. Southwards, the summits of Nilgiri and Tilicho loom.

▮▮ **DAY 2**: The trail leaves the village and stays on the river's east side. After crossing the confluence of the Gyalungbo, the trail reaches the village of Tangbe around midday, an ideal spot for lunch. The trail winds its way through the village to reach a group of settlements, Chusang. Those who can afford an extra day may want to stay there to explore a castle and a few prehistoric dwellings. The trail crosses the confluence of Narsing Khola with Kali Gandaki and comes out of the valley, climbing steeply, to reach Tsaili (10,007 ft / 3,050 m) village.

▮I DAY 3: This day is a little tough as it involves climbing five passes, though not of substantial heights. Leave early for the climb to the Chotare Lampach pass. The trail then descends to Samar village located among poplar trees lining irrigation canals. Descend to cross a stream and follow the trail climbing to Samar La. The trail descends again, goes past a few houses and ascends to another small pass. Descend and the trail reaches Yamda. The next trip is the climb to Dawa Lapcha pass (12,697 ft / 3,870 m) marked by a large cairn and prayer flags. Descend to Syangmuche; avail of the brew at its teashop and then climb to Lhakpa La (12,665 ft / 3,860 m), the last pass for the day. The trail reaches a fork after coming down the pass. Now take the upper trail to reach the Tamang settlement of Tamaghyang.

▮I DAY 4: Go up to Chaiti and up again to the Tstil La. Descend to the next fork and take the upper trail to reach Gemi village for lunch. The trail keeps to the left of the village and

goes through two passes to reach the Tramar (also, Trakmar) village. There are some great views of Gemi and Damodar Himal from the passes. And you are in Upper Mustang.

▮I DAY 5: The destination is Lo-Manthang, the ancient capital of Mustang, where the king still resides. A steep, one-hour climb north-east of Tramar gets you to the top of the plateau. Crossing it, you reach a small pass and descend to Marang village. The ancient temple of Lo Gekar has excellent samples of rock slate paintings. The inner chamber also houses statues of Padmasambhava and Milarepa. The trail then climbs via a pass to the north pastures, reaching the base of a long pass overlooking the Lo Manthang valley. Another hour brings you to the walled city. Across the city, the Tibetan plateau shimmers in the distance and the Damodar peak looks on from the right.

▮I DAY 6: Spend the day exploring Lo-Manthang. Mustang is probably a mispronunciation of Manthang in Nepalese, which means Plains of Aspiration or Plains of Prayer. Mustang has come to signify the entire district south of the Tibetan border along the Kali Gandaki till Ghasa. It's the region north of Kagbeni, Upper Mustang, that the traveller looks for. Manthang presents a contradiction articulated in its two monasteries: Thubchen Gompa represents the practical and rational side of Buddhism; Chamba Gompa signifies

▮I Rhododendrons

the mystical side. The third monastery, Chodi, belongs to the Sakya sect and forms the monks' residential quarters. The Namgyal monastery is also there above a village with the same name.

▮I DAY 7: A week into the trip, this day can be spent as a rest day. Or you could go on an excursion to the villages of Gharphu and Nyphu, north of Manthang. There are stunning cave monasteries there with dwellings inside. A short return hike takes you to the ruins of the Ketcher Fortress.

▮I DAYS 8-9: A minor detour on the way back brings you to Dri village on the banks of the Mustang Khola. A steep climb takes you to camp at Yara village. On the ninth day, climb to the village of Gara, on way to the cave monastery of Luri. It's built inside the sandstone cliffs with a chapel and an inner room that contains a stupa embellished with deities. The monastery is supposed to have been built by Guru Padmasambhava. Return to Diri camp in the evening.

▮I DAYS 10-13: Returning to the main trail, reach Tsarang, an important town with a large monastery and palace that once housed the king. Continue south along the main trail, with a side trip to a meditation cave used by Guru Padmasambhava. Set deep in a juniper-clad valley, this cave with its self-emanated rock images and spiritual aura adds to the journey. The last day of trekking brings one back to Jomsom.

▮I DAY 14: Fly from Jomsom to Pokhara.

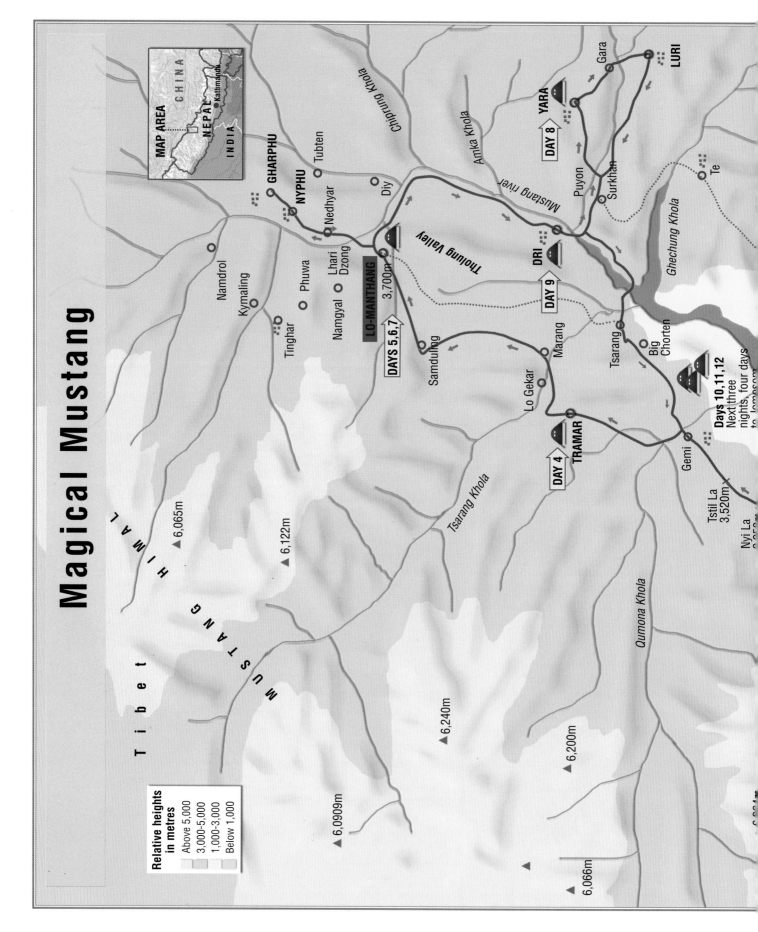

Magical Mustang

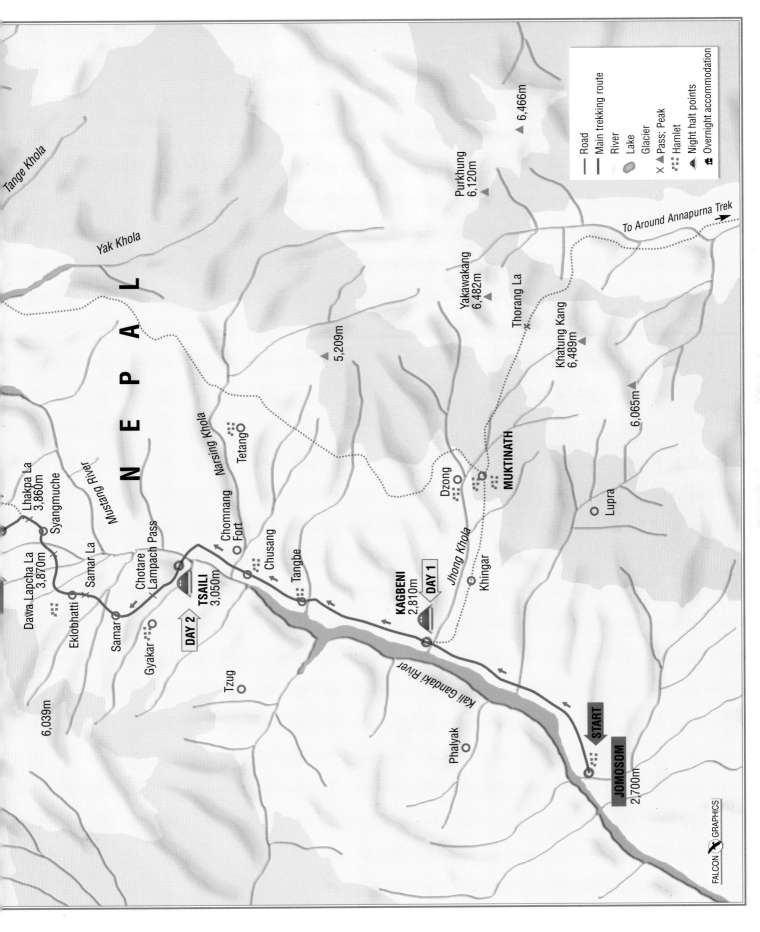

■ The meadow of Shana, and the Bandarpunch peaks in the background; facing page: A villager from Wan

5

Land of Gods: Kumaon and Garhwal

THE Uttaranchal/Uttarakhand region of the Himalaya abounds with captivating myths about its charms, its omniscient divinities, and the sages who travelled there to look for salvation. It is known as *dev bhoomi* or the Land of the Gods. Not only as the point of origin for the rivers that have shaped the economic destiny of the Indian plains, but also as the fountainhead of wisdom that has defined moral perceptions, Uttaranchal has always been a significant part of the collective Indian consciousness.

Situated between Himachal Pradesh and the border of eastern Nepal in central Himalaya, Uttaranchal or the Northern Region has been an important pilgrimage place for the Hindus. It has a rich past though it has evolved as two distinct entities, Garhwal and Kumaon, with different languages and heritages. They still share a lot in terms of religion and social structure.

The Katyuri dynasty of Kumaon ruled Uttaranchal between the eighth and fourteenth centuries. Art and architecture flourished under the Katyuris and the exquisite temples at Baijnath, Joshimath, and Jageshwar are a testimony to their contribution. With the disintegration of this dynasty, Kumaon and Garhwal followed different courses. The Chand dynasty with its capital at Almora ruled supreme in Kumaon as did the Panwars in Garhwal with their capital at Srinagar. At the end of the eighteenth century, however, a consolidated Gurkha campaign from Nepal eroded the supremacy of the local rulers and by 1803, Uttaranchal had fallen to sustained assault from the east.

By this time, the British had become vital players. After a series of bloody battles they pushed the Gurkha army back to the Mahakali river and fixed the Nepal border at this natural line of demarcation. Restoring the Tehri Garhwal area to the raja, the British took control of the rest of Garhwal and of Kumaon. Soon the Garhwalis and the Kumaonis became important pillars of the empire.

Recently, developmental issues fed a sustained agitation for a separate hill state. The movement received great popular support. Finally, in 2000, the region became a separate state, Uttaranchal.

Uttaranchal has suffered as regards the marketing of its great beauty and has remained a poor cousin to Nepal, the Himalaya and even the Karakorams. But its mountains abound with pretty valleys, verdant jungles, luxuriant meadows, and an impressive assembly of peaks. The valleys receive huge amounts of rain and have a great variety of vegetation. With increasing population, the forest cover has been damaged. The thick jungles of Kumaon where Jim Corbett hunted man-eaters are wastelands bereft of trees; rivers have dried up, and landslides and flash floods have become frequent. But such is the bounty of nature in the region that huge areas still lie untouched by human hands. There are dense jungles where you would have to hack your way through. The sheer vertical faces of peaks like Changabang and Swargarohini are not the highest in the world but can test the mettle of the best mountaineers.

....

Trek I   Roop Kund-Kuari Pass-Tapovan

■I Roop Kund, the mystery lake, during the Nanda Devi Jat Yatra

Ways & Means

Duration:
13 days

Degree of Difficulty
3 to 4: Moderate to rigorous

Getting There
There are two driving options:
Two days of driving from Delhi, with an overnight stay at Almora, brings you to the village of Mandoli, the road head.
You could also drive from Delhi to Karanprayag, via Rishikesh, and from there to Mandoli. This will also take two days, but is better connected by local buses. Or take an overnight bus from Delhi to Karanprayag and get a connecting bus to Mandoli.
From Tapovan at the end of the trek, an hour's drive will get you to Joshimath. From here a long twenty hours by bus could get you to Delhi. You could stay overnight at Rishikesh to break the journey.

Best Time
End-March to end-June (till the start of the monsoons), and again from mid-September to mid-December (depending on the onset of winter snows).

Altitude
Mandoli at 6,000 ft / 1,829 m. The highest point reached is Roop Kund at 16,500 ft / 5,029 m and Kuari Pass at 14,003 ft / 4,268 m. The highest campsite is at Bedni Bugyal, 11,004 ft / 3,354 m.

Highlights
Spectacular meadows of Ali Bugyal and Bedni Bugyal; Roop Kund – the mystery lake! One of the best mountain views in the entire Himalaya, of the entire outer Nanda Devi Sanctuary, can be seen from Kuari Pass.

Support Services
Porters and cooking staff easily available at Joshimath at the end of the trek. Arrange for these services in advance so that porters can reach Mandoli in time. Limited porters also available at Mandoli. Guest houses available at many campsites but almost no food, except in villages like Wan and Sutol. Be self-equipped for almost the entire trek.
Almora, Rishikesh, Karanprayag and Joshimath have good hotels.

Emergency
Hardly any medical facilities throughout the trip except Joshimath. Helicopter rescue available but very hard to arrange. Telephone communication available in many larger villages.

■| Skeletal remains at the Roop Kund Lake are seen when the snow thaws.

Hundreds of years ago on a cold, windy night, some unfortunate souls froze to death on the shores of an isolated high altitude lake in Uttaranchal. Since the discovery of their skeletal remains, speculation has grown on whether they were part of a retreating army of traders or simple pilgrims. But nothing has been concluded. The bones remain a chilling reminder of the fickle ways of nature: charming and serene at one moment, sinister and deadly the next, and unforgiving to those who underestimate its might.

Straddling the border between the regions of Garhwal and Kumaon, the Roop Kund-Kuari Pass trek winds its way through some of the most picturesque areas of Uttaranchal. With entry to the natural sanctuary at the base of Nanda Devi being banned, this is an alternate route that takes you to the west of the peak. An eighteen-hour drive from Delhi brings you to

Roop Kund-Kuari Pass-Tapovan

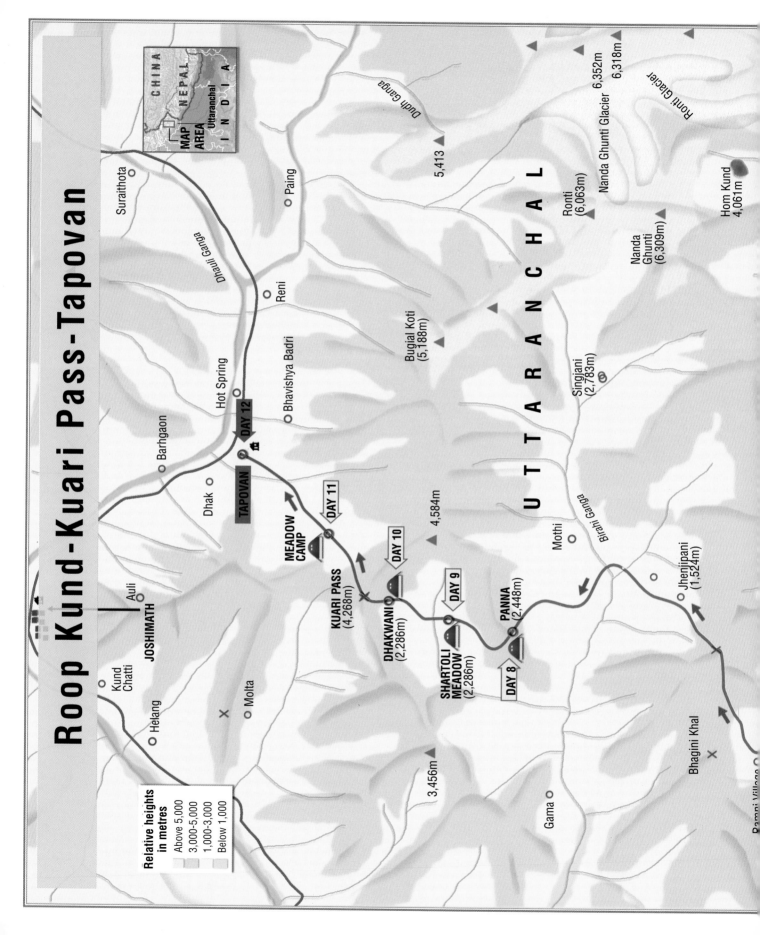

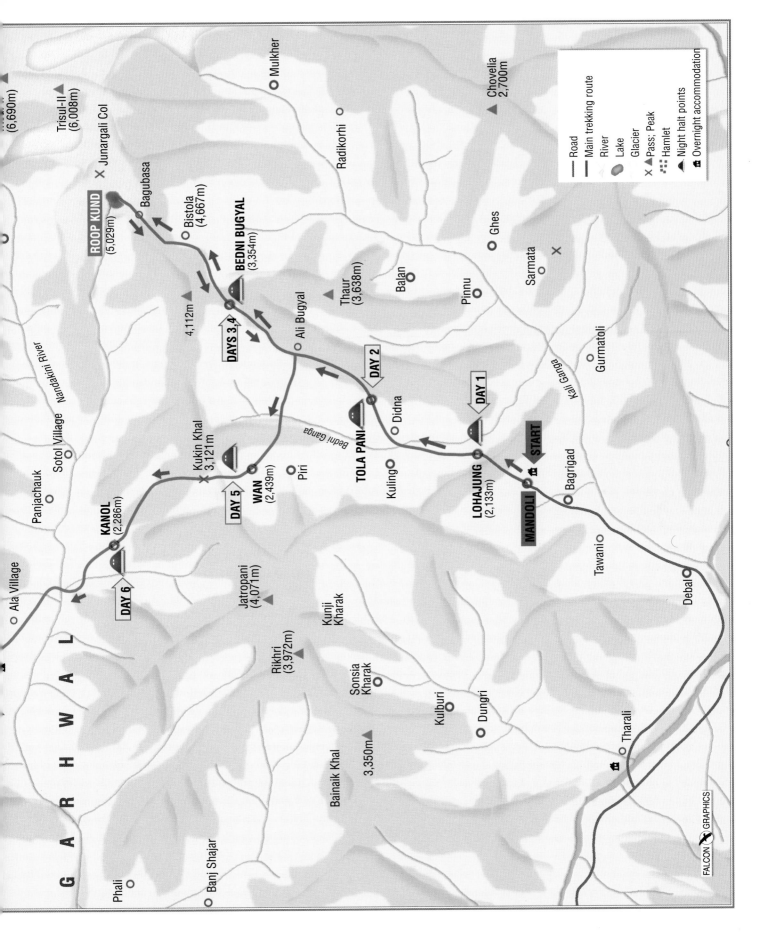

Nanda Ghunti peak (20,703 ft / 6,310 m)

Mandoli, the road head for the Roop Kund-Kuari pass trek, with a night halt at Almora, Kumaon's erstwhile capital.

DAY 1: The hike is a short one keeping in view the last two days' tiring drive. A steep one-hour climb leads to Lohajung village (7,045 ft / 2,147 m), with the Pindar river valley to the south and Trisul and Nanda Ghunti peaks to the north. Pitch camp next to the forest rest house. Icing Top, a pretty pasture, is a four-hour walk away with excellent views.

DAY 2: A walk descends through a dense oak forest to a stream. Cross over to the other side of the valley, and climb for an hour and a half to reach the open meadow of Meldhar. Another hour's walk brings you to the Neelganga river. The trail crosses over and after a steep climb of an hour and a half, you reach the small village of Didna. Continuing to climb through thick forests of pine, rhododendron, and oak for another ninety minutes, the trail reaches the campsite at the idyllic pastoral setting of Tola Pani (8,800 ft / 2,682 m), which is the summer grazing ground for the people of Didna.

DAY 3: Now the trail crosses the meadow to the left and keeps following the ridge northwards. From the ridge, you get a lovely view of the Jatropani range with the alpine lakes of Brahma Tal and Bhegal Tal shimmering at its base. After an hour's climb on the ridge, you reach the alpine meadow of Khurtal (11,000 ft / 3,653 m). This is a heavenly place with a gorgeous view of the Neelganga valley to the north-west, with the towering summits of Chaukhamba, Neelkanth, and Kedarnath beckoning from the upper Ganga valley, and picture postcard views of the villages of Didna, Kulin, and Wan below in the valley. This is classic Uttaranchal country. Another climb through a rhododendron forest takes you to the meadows of Ali Bugyal rolling on for almost 3.5 km to join the equally magnificent meadows of Bedni Bugyal (11,004 ft / 3,354 m), where the campsite is situated next to

a little lake called Bedni Kund. On the way between the two meadows, you get spectacular views of the summits of Nanda Ghunti, Trisul, and Hathi Parbat.

DAY 4: Take the day trip to Roop Kund. The trail climbs up to the Pathar Nachauni ridge to get closer views of Trisul, Nanda Ghunti, and Changabang, one of the toughest peaks in the Indian Himalaya. A steep zigzag brings you to the caves of Balpa Sulera where the locals have made rock-shelters for people to spend the night. Another five-hour climb over scree and rocks and you reach Roop Kund (16,500 ft / 5,029 m), in the eerie presence of skeletons buried in the snow if you are there in early summer. Carbon dating has revealed they are almost six hundred years old. Hurry back on the steep descent to the comfort of Bedni Bugyal camp.

DAY 5: You are on a short downhill descent to the charming Wan village (8,003 ft / 2,439 m). Through a thick forest, traversing the mountainside brings you to the Neelganga coming down from its origin at Bedni Kund. Crossing over, a short climb takes you to Wan nestled in a semi-bowl-shaped valley. The forest rest house where you can set up camp is a fifteen-minute climb up the village.

DAY 6: The trail leaves the village to climb up through the fields and an ascent leads to the small pass of Kukin Khal on an open meadow. Walking through grassland, descend to Kanol

■| Bedni Bugyal meadow with the peaks of Chaukhamba (23,426 ft / 7,140 m) and Neelkanth (21,655 ft / 6,600 m)

village (7,828 ft / 2,386 m) where you can again pitch camp, next to the rest house.

■| **DAY 7**:The trail descends steeply through a thick pine forest and down to a small stream, which is then followed all the way down to the Nandakini river. Follow the river upstream for fifteen minutes; cross over to the right bank and begin a long, steep climb. There are several trails here and you could easily get lost. A three-hour climb through fields and mixed forests, switchbacking up

the mountainside brings you to Ala village. After a fifteen-minute descent followed by a steep ninety-minute ascent, you reach the meadows of Bora (8,500 ft / 2,590 m) at the ridge top where you can pitch camp.

■| **DAY 8**: Another undulating trek. A short descent followed by a forty-five-minute climb brings you to Pander. After a steady three-and-a-half hour climb through a dense forest, you reach a junction of trails at the ridge top. The trail descends for ten minutes to reach an open meadow from where you get

the first views of the Kuari Pass. Descending two hours through a dense forest, you are at Jhinjhi village. Across the valley, see today's destination, Panna village. The trail descends to the valley floor to cross the Behri Ganga that drains the western slopes of Nanda Ghunti. A final ascent of around two and a half hours leads to Panna village (8,032 ft / 2,448 m). After an hour's walk into the valley, past a waterfall, you hit the campsite.

■| **DAY 9**: An hour's climb through open pastures, followed by a steep climb through a dense forest for almost two and a half hours, brings you to the ridge top. Keeping the forest to the right, the trail goes along the ridge for just under thirty minutes and descends around 200 ft to the campsite at the Shartoli pastures (11,300 ft / 2,444 m). The campsite has a water problem and water has to be fetched from a stream forty-five minutes away.

■ DAY 10: A slow descent of about forty-five minutes brings you to a hump from where a descent through rubble on a broken trail leads to a waterfall. Jump over rocks to the other side, and take the trail climbing steeply through the forest. Descend to the Dhakwani Nallah coming down

the Kuari Pass, and cross over to climb steeply for two-and-a-half hours through rhododendron forests to reach the grasslands of Dhakwani ·(11,700 ft / 3,566 m) at the base of Kuari Pass.

■ DAY 11: Today's your date with Kuari Pass. Over the years this place has suffered due to erosion and landslides. Though earlier the trail used to go up a grassland all the way to the top, these days loose rubble hinders your way. A steep two-hour climb from Dhakwani brings you to the top of the Pass (14,003 ft / 4,268 m). There's a gigantic sweep of icy peaks in front of you, some of the giants of Uttaranchal: Kamet, Kedarnath, Badrinath, Hathi Parbat, Dunagiri,

Neelkanth, and in the distance, the reigning queen, the Goddess Nanda Devi. Descend 500 ft to a stream coming down from the top of the Pass to set up camp.

■ DAY 12: The trail circles around the meadows below the Pass, descending to enter the forest. A four-hour steep descent through rhododendron, oak, and pine forests takes you to Kulari village. The trail then crosses the Kulari Nallah and goes along it till it reaches a small canal emerging from the Nallah. An hour's walk brings you to a hump overlooking the Dhauli Ganga valley with a great view of Dunagiri Peak across the river. Just below, next to the road, is the Tapovan village. The trek is over.

Nanda Devi Raj Yatra

EVERY 12 years, a ceremonial religious procession comes to Roop Kund from the village of Nauti, north of Karanprayag, to propitiate Goddess Nanda Devi. Popularly known as the Nanda Devi Raj Jat Yatra, the procession is led by a four-horned ram and consists of several silver images of Nanda Devi carried in palanquins. Sombre priests, devout holy men and thousands of merry villagers accompany the *Yatra*. Pujas and rituals are performed at the lake and then the *Yatra* climbs up the steep Jiura Gali down to the lush meadows of the Nandakini valley. Further up in the valley is Hom Kund, the destination of the *Yatra*. Here the ram is released and the locals believe that immediately after, it mysteriously disappears. The last *Yatra* took place in 2000.

Trek II

Corbett Park-Nainital

The trekking season in Uttaranchal is confined to summer and autumn as the inner areas remain inaccessible through winter and spring. The heavy snowfall experienced in these seasons makes walking almost impossible. A fun-filled, four-day trek could take you to the hills after a sojourn at Corbett National Park in the foothills. The uniqueness of this trek is that the trail goes through the jungle terrain of the Shivaliks first, then winds its way up to mixed deciduous forests of oak, chestnut, and bamboo to finally reach thick pine forests above Nainital. Frequently, you see the Indian plains on one side and get distant glimpses of the Himalayan peaks to the north.

Flowing through the northern parts of the park, the Ramganga is Corbett's lifeline and also acts as a vital drainage outlet for the park. An earthen dam (the largest in Asia) was built on the river in the mid-'70s. It inundated nearly sixteen square kilometres of prime habitat within the park. The lake formed by the dam draws a large number of water birds including migrants from Siberia. The number of crocodiles has also increased. The park was known as Ramganga National Park for a brief period from 1952 to 1957. In 1957, the park was rechristened after the legendary naturalist Jim Corbett. In the '30s, it was he who had demarked the park's boundaries and worked closely with the British authorities to set it up.

Ways & Means

Duration
4 days

Degree of Difficulty
1 to 2: Easy to moderate. Only one day involves a steep climb.

Getting There
Corbett Park is near the town of Ramnagar in the new state of Uttaranchal. It is well connected by road, and by rail from Moradabad only. Nainital is well connected by road. The nearest rail head is at Kathgodam which is linked with the rest of the country, especially Delhi.

Best Time
From November to April in the cooler months, though December and January can be very cold.

Altitude
The starting point for the trek at Patkot village outside of Corbett Park is only at 1,200 ft / 366 m. The highest point is Kunjakharak at just over 7,000 ft / 2,134 m or Vinayak at 7,300 ft / 2,225 m.

Highlights
Excellent bird watching; great views from Bhameshwar of the Corbett Park forest and from Kunjakharak of the Himalayan peaks; connects two of the most popular tourist destinations in the Indian Himalaya.

Support Services
Guides and porters available in Patkot village but must be arranged for in advance, or time must be allowed for this arrangement as very few trekkers visit here. Lots of very good accommodation available in Corbett and Nainital but almost none on the trail. Very basic guest house at Kunjakharak and Vinayak. At Bhameshwar temple one or two people could stay with the priest! But do carry some food for a couple of days.

Emergency
Reasonable medical facilities available only at Nainital and to some extent in Ramnagar. Telephone link available at Kunjakharak and Vinayak. A dirt road leads from Kunjakharak to Vinayak and then there is a metal road to Nainital. The trek route does not follow this metal road, but drops down the mountain by a short cut, straight to Nainital.

■I The final descent to Nainital

Spread out for 520 sq km with a core sanctum of 320 sq km, Corbett is a unique wilderness area. The valley and the lower ridges are forested with sal trees and the riverine area has a profusion of teak. The higher ridges have *chir* pine and a pretty red-leafed tree locally known as *bakli*. The grasslands abound with grasses where the tiger hunts. The spotted deer or *chital* is the most noticeable denizen. Hog deer, barking deer, and the majestic sambar are the other deer species. *Goral*, a species of goat-antelopes, is found on the craggy hillsides. Civets, martens, mongoose, pangolins, porcupines, linsangs, and hares are some smaller mammals. Sloth bears are found in the forest and the rocky terrain and Himalayan black bears can be seen on the higher reaches in the winters. Leopard cats, jungle cats, fishing cats, and leopards are the predatory species. The prime attractions of Corbett, however, are the elephant and the tiger. With a population of nearly three hundred, Corbett is one of the last refuges for Asiatic elephants in north India. Consuming 200 kg of green fodder daily and wasting around the same, an elephant makes severe demands on its habitat. Corbett can sustain the beast due to its rich vegetation. A thriving elephant population also indicates a healthy ecosystem.

■I **DAY 1**: Proceed on the unmetalled road just outside the main gate of the Corbett Park down to the Kosi river to enter the Sitabani Reserve Forest. A ninety-minute drive through a sal and teak forest brings you to Patkot village (1,200 ft / 366 m) at the edge of the forest where the hills begin. The trek starts from the village. The initial gradual climb takes you through a thick growth of lantana bushes, a weed that has been a cause of concern for many wilderness areas. A hardy plant, lantana grows easily and smothers all the shrubs around it. Nothing symbolises a degraded habitat as much as these bushes. Soon you enter a thick sal forest to descend to the Kalagarh stream. The path climbs up steeply just short of a wooden bridge, again through a sal forest, to Amtoli village. After a short break, climb up steeply on the face of a barren hill. With a high demand for fuel-wood, trees in the lower hills of Kumaon and Garhwal have been religiously felled, resulting in massive soil erosion. The siltation caused by this on river and stream beds leads to disastrous floods.

The trail climbs up the barren hill to reach the shepherd settlement of Bineka. Traversing the hillside through an oak forest, reach the campsite at the Bhameshwar temple (4,900 ft / 1,493 m) dedicated to Shiva, which dates back to eight hundred years. At almost 5,000 ft, Corbett Park lies sprawled below you and the plains further beyond.

■I **DAY 2**: It begins with a steep climb through a thick oak forest to cross a small pass on the ridge. A two-hour walk from the camp brings you to Bhagini village. You are in typical hill country going through a dense forest of oak, chestnut, and bamboo with a few rhododendron trees. Staying just below the Devidhara ridge, the trail climbs steadily for three hours to Kultani village where there is a break in the ridge. In another hour, you reach the Kunjakharak forest rest house (7,000 ft / 2,134 m) situated in a reserved forest. From the watch-tower close to the rest house you see the Nanda Devi complex shimmering in the north. Carry a few empty jerrycans as water sources are not always near campsites or rest houses.

▮ **DAY 3**: The walk is easy as you follow a wide unmetalled road through a dense forest. Going along the ridge, the road stays almost level. This is a great day for bird-watching. If you are there in spring, the migratory birds would be back. Thrushes, chats, minivets, sunbirds, warbles, sparrows, woodpeckers, skylarks, and parakeets can be seen. A leisurely five-hour walk from the camp leads to Vinayak Rest House (7,300 ft / 2,225 m).

▮ **DAY 4**: The last day is another unhurried trek through some thick pine forest. At the end of the first six kilometres stretch comes Pangot village. From there a smaller trail descends to Nainital, fifteen kilometres away. The approach to the town is from the top of the Naina hill, presenting a great top view. The view suddenly opens up to a fabulous natural amphitheatre of wooded hills enclosing the pretty, banana-shaped lake below. A trail snakes its way down to the town. As the chill descends in the evening, it's time for some hot rum next to a fireplace in a room overlooking Naini lake.

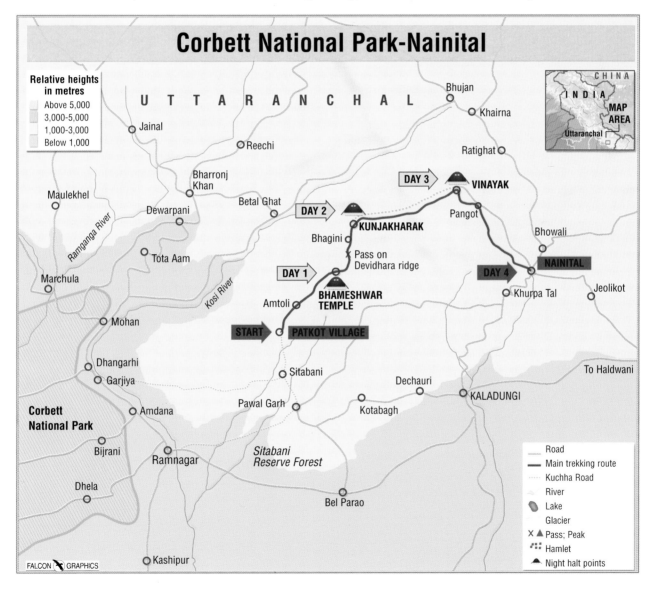

Trek III   Gangotri-Gaumukh-Tapovan

ar removed from the world of science lies the path to Gaumukh or the Cow's Mouth, from where the waters of the Gangotri Glacier gush out to create the waters of the Ganga, India's holy river. People in advanced stages of terminal diseases, infirm matrons and disabled men gingerly tread this pilgrim path in search of salvation. It's a trail that is somewhat crowded and standards of sanitation are low, but for a trekker looking for communion with the dignity of the human spirit, the Gangotri-Gaumukh trek is an experience of a lifetime. This route also passes through a dramatic setting of towering peaks, majestic glaciers and high-altitude meadows.

A twelve-hour drive from Delhi leads to Uttarkashi on the Bhagirathi river, which you will follow all the way to Gangotri on the next day's drive. Ganga is known as Bhagirathi, after the king whose penance coaxed her down from heaven. Frequent glimpses of the shimmering Sudarshan Peak at the valley head give you solace that your destination is getting closer on this nerve-racking journey. Gangotri (10,303 ft / 3,140 m) is a largish village with a modest Goddess Ganga temple and many ashrams and *dharamsalas* (tourist hostels within temple complexes) that cater to pilgrims and holy men. Ascetics, renunciates, and hermits stay there all through the summer months.

▮ⅼ The approach to the peaks of Thalay Sagar (22,652 ft / 6,904 m) and Bhrigupanth (22,219 ft / 6,772 m)

Ways & Means

Duration
8 days

Degree of Difficulty
3 to 4: Moderate to rigorous (only because of the altitude gained, otherwise the day hikes are quite easy)

Getting There
The bus journey begins from Rishikesh. It is well connected by road. A one-hour drive short of Rishikesh is the pilgrimage town of Haridwar, linked by rail too. A six-hour bus journey leads to Uttarkashi; another bus journey reaches Gangotri, the road head, in not more than eight hours.

Best Time
April to early July and again from mid-September to end-November or later, depending on the onset of winter snows.

Altitude
Gangotri is at 10,303 ft / 3,140 m and Tapovan, the highest campsite, is at 14,643 ft / 4,463 m. The highest altitude gained depends on how far the day hikes take you from Tapovan and from Nandanvan, probably up to 16,000 ft / 4,900 m.

Highlights
Gangotri attracts a crowd especially during pilgrimage time. Follow pilgrims all the way to Gaumukh, and the mendicant who travels even further up the glacier. The huge waterfall at Gangotri, the spectacular mountain vistas from Tapovan, the huge Gangotri Glacier with its ribbons of ice, are attractions.

Support Services
Porters can be hired at Gangotri, though during pilgrimage time the rates can be quite high. Various travel agents in Uttarkashi will do the hiring for you in advance for a small commission, or even do all the rest of the trekking arrangements. No facilities are available beyond Gaumukh. Therefore, be self-equipped. Even up to Gaumukh, the accommodation available is very basic and some tea houses provide basic food only. Gangotri has reasonable guest houses and hotels but they must be booked in advance.

Emergency
Basic medical facilities are available in Uttarkashi and some in Gangotri. The army bases on the way at Lanka and Harsil also have some facilities. Rescue facilities are available but difficult to arrange. The last communication link is from the ashram at Bhojbasa.

█▌ DAY 1: Leaving the holy village behind on the first day, a four-hour hike on an easy gradient takes you to Chirbasa or The Pine Grove. Set amid the *chir* pine trees, the campsite is ideal. The gigantic Gangotri Glacier glistens ahead while herds of blue sheep graze on the hills.

█▌ DAY 2: The trail goes past Bhojbasa (The Birch Grove) where Lal Baba, an ascetic much respected for his service to the pilgrims, offers free food and shelter at his ashram. Just beyond the ashram you get the first views of the Bhagirathi peaks. The valley continues to curve southwards above Bhojbasa. Most dramatic is the emergence of the conical summit of the Shivling Peak (21,470 ft / 6,543 m). After an hour's walk from Bhojbasa you reach Gaumukh, the snout of the Gangotri at the end of the valley. Almost twenty-five kilometres long, the Gangotri Glacier is the longest in the southern Indian Himalaya (Siachen in the Karakoram is sixty-five kilometres long). Pilgrims take a dip in the chilling waters as the three peaks of the Bhagirathi complex tower over the springs.

█▌ DAY 3: The walk begins with a steep climb on a scree slope to the left of the Gangotri Glacier. At the end of the slope, cross over to the Glacier's right. That will take almost an hour and a half. Another hour and you reach Tapovan (14,643 ft / 4,463 m). It's another twenty minutes to the camping site. The perspective on Shivling keeps changing, the summit turning more pointed. From Tapovan,

Gangotri-Gaumukh-Tapovan

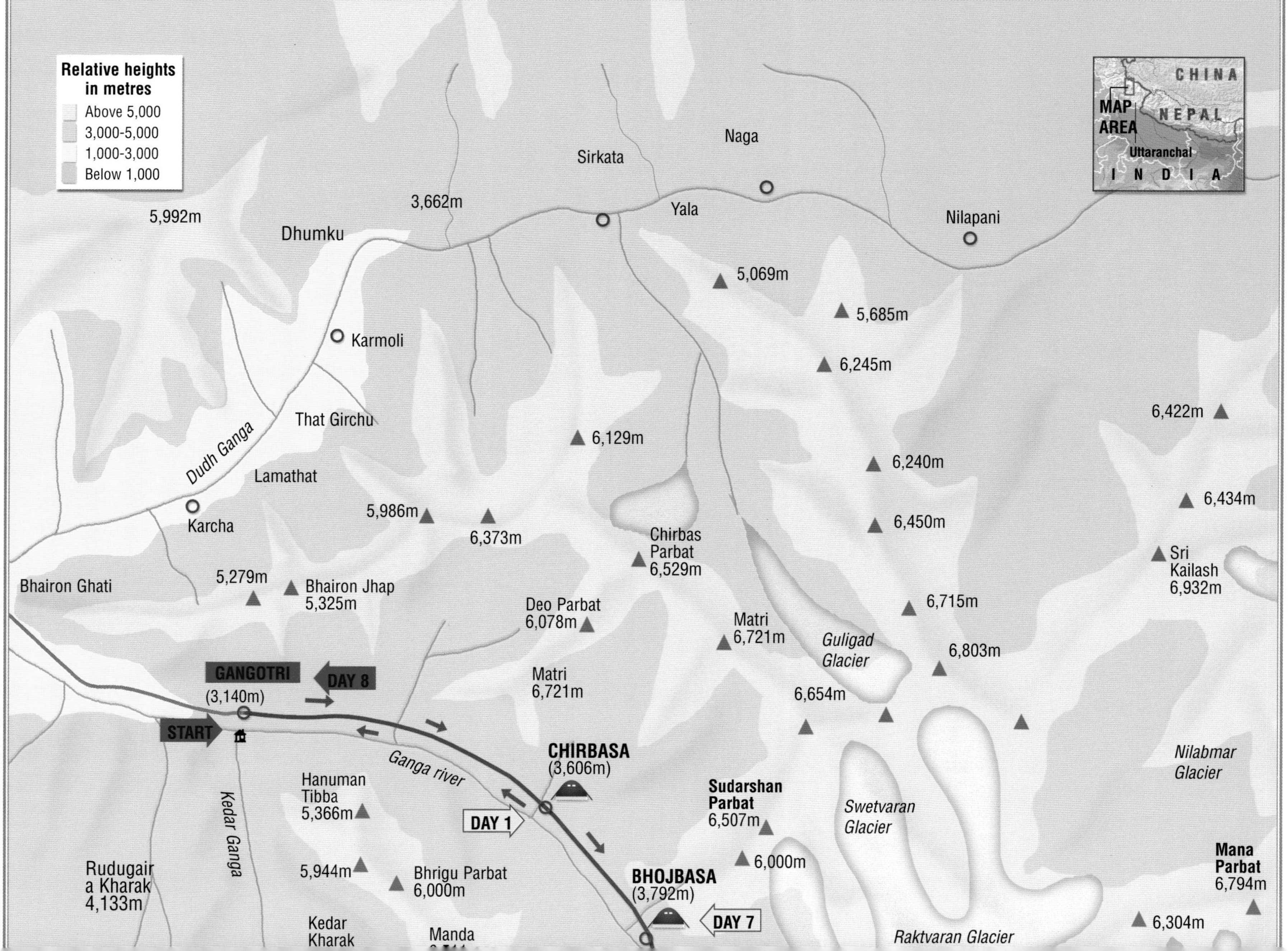

Relative heights in metres

Above 5,000
3,000-5,000
1,000-3,000
Below 1,000

MAP AREA

CHINA
NEPAL
INDIA
Uttaranchal

Mana Parbat 6,794m

6,304m

6,434m

Sri Kailash 6,932m

6,422m

Nilabmar Glacier

Raktvaran Glacier

6,803m

6,715m

6,450m

6,240m

5,685m

Swetvaran Glacier

Guligad Glacier

6,654m

6,000m

Sudarshan Parbat 6,507m

Matri 6,721m

Chirbas Parbat 6,529m

6,129m

6,245m

5,069m

Nilapani

Naga

Yala

Sirkata

3,662m

Dhumku

5,992m

Karmoli

That Girchu

Lamathat

Karcha

5,279m

5,986m

Bhairon Jhap 5,325m

6,373m

Deo Parbat 6,078m

Matri 6,721m

BHOJBASA (3,792m)

DAY 7

CHIRBASA (3,606m)

DAY 1

Ganga river

Hanuman Tibba 5,366m

Bhrigu Parbat 6,000m

5,944m

Kedar Kharak

Manda

DAY 8

GANGOTRI (3,140m)

START

Kedar Ganga

Rudugair a Kharak 4,133m

Duдh Ganga

Bhairon Ghati

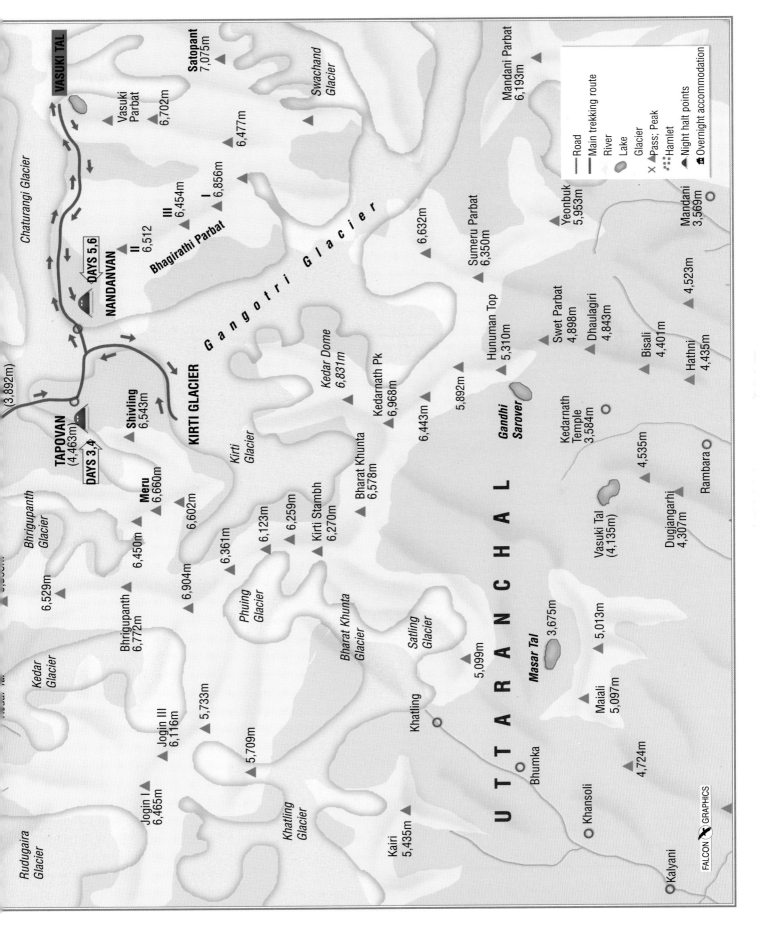

witness the spectacle of the sun's rays beaming down on a magnificent theatre of snow-capped peaks. Immediately to the right is Bhrigupanth (22,219 ft / 6,772 m) and Meru (21,851 ft / 6,660 m) next to it. To the left of Shivling lie Bhagirathi II (21,360 ft / 6,512 m), III (21,176 ft / 6,454 m), and I (22,495 ft / 6,856 m), and beyond them the tip of Satopant (23,213 ft / 7,075 m). As you turn around to look north, Mana Parbat (22,291 ft / 6,794 m) and Shri Kailash (22,745 ft / 6,932 m) loom up on the horizon. Towards Gangotri town to your south, Sudarshan (21,350 ft / 6,507 m) continues its vigil.

■ **DAY 4**: Keeping camp at Tapovan, take a forty-five-minute walk to the ridge top. It offers an overview of the majestic Gangotri Glacier sprawled below you. Follow the ridge up to the confluence of the Gangotri Glacier with Kirti Glacier to view Kedarnath (22,862 ft / 6,968 m) on your right, Satopant on the left, and Gangotri tumbling down between the two.

■ **DAYS 5, 6**: A four-hour walk brings you to Nandanvan. Cross over to the glacier's right and walk on a lateral moraine next to it for two hours. The glacier reaches the edge of the Tapovan meadow. A thirty-minute walk takes you to the confluence of the Chaturangi (Four Colour) Glacier and the Gangotri Glacier. Cross the former to reach the Nandanvan meadows dominated by the summit of Bhagirathi III. Explore Vasuki Tal. Follow the Chaturangi Glacier on its left bank to reach the base of Vasuki Parbat (22,275 ft / 6,789 m), where the lake is. Climb up from the lake to get breathtaking views of Satopant and Mana Parbat. This is another great place for blue sheep.

■ **DAY 7**: Descend straight to Bhojbasa from Nandanvan. Start descending from the moraine on the right of the Gangotri Glacier to reach Gaumukh in three-and-a-half hours. Another two hours on the pilgrim route takes you to Bhojbasa.

■ **DAY 8**: You are back at Gangotri village quite convinced that a place as stunningly beautiful as the upper Gangotri valley would tempt the Gods to come and frolic in the meadows and snow slopes.

A horse, a thousand souls and the Ganga

WHEN the Himalaya were quite young, a mighty king called Sagar waged war against all evil and triumphed against the demons. To prove his supremacy, he performed the Ashwamedha Yagya or Horse Sacrifice: an army escorted a horse through surrounding kingdoms and those who interfered with its wanderings had to battle with the army. King Sagar's horse was escorted by his 60,000 sons. Indra, the king of all gods, saw this *yagya* as a threat, fearing its completion would make Sagar a competitor for the celestial throne. He stole the horse and tied it to a post at the hermitage of Sage Kapil, known for his mercurial temperament. Searching for the horse, King Sagar's sons reached the hermitage and were about to attack it when Sage Kapil, disturbed in his meditation, opened an eye to reduce the army to ashes. Only one son survived the sage's wrath. The survivor's son, Anshuman, performed a penance to recover the horse and attain salvation for his uncles. Kapil returned the horse but said the souls of the dead could be saved only if Goddess Ganga descended from the heavens to cleanse their ashes. It was difficult for anyone used to the pleasures of heaven to come down to earth, and so was it with Ganga. Anshuman and then, his son Dilip, spent their lifetimes propitiating Ganga, but failed. Anshuman's grandson King Bhagirath, however, won the gods over by his determined penance and they agreed to Ganga's descent. There was, however, another issue to be sorted out. Ganga's mighty flow could wreak havoc if it hit the earth directly. Bhagirath now propitiated Lord Shiva to receive the stormy waters on His head. Pleased by his devotion, Shiva agreed, and Ganga descended on the earth.

Due to this myth, the Ganga's waters are considered absolutely pure, and on his death bed a Hindu is administered a few drops so that his soul can enter heaven. People go on a pilgrimage to the source of Ganga at Gaumukh and even ■ Phlomis today renunciates make a beeline to spend their lives in this tough but enchanting place.

Trek IV

Ruinsara Tal-Har Ki Dun-Yamnotri

Ways & Means

All through human history the achievements of a few have created new paths for many. The climbing of Everest by Tenzing and Hillary in 1953 infused enthusiasm among Indian youth to go and explore the Himalaya. Tenzing Norgay, a Sherpa by origin but an Indian by citizenship, became a folk-hero whose exploits in the mountains acquired a mythical tinge in the schools and colleges of the plains. The Indian expedition of 1965 placed nine summitteers atop Everest, and soon there were youngsters trooping off to the Himalaya. The Tons valley, where Har Ki Dun and Ruinsara Tal are situated, became a favourite stomping ground for trekkers because of its easy accessibility to Delhi, Chandigarh, and Dehradun.

A ten-hour drive from Dehradun takes you to Sankri (4,757 ft / 1,450 m), the road head. The road winds its way through the Garhwal hinterland to reach Netwar (4,578 ft / 1,380 m), the confluence of Rupin and Supin rivers that forms the Tons. Sankri is a short drive away from Netwar, and it is advisable to stay overnight at the forest rest house there. Next day begin the trek after an early morning drive.

■ **DAY 1**: A three-hour walk on a level dirt track brings you to Taluka (6,234 ft / 1,900 m) village. The campsite is an hour away from Taluka, below the village of Datmi. Walk on the left bank of the Supin river with forested hillsides around you.

Duration

13 days of walking

Degree of Difficulty

4: Moderate to rigorous

Getting There

Dehradun is well connected by road and rail. From there a ten-hour drive leads to Netwar, the road head. A dirt road leads further to Sankri and Taluka. At the end of the trek from Hanuman Chatti, there are buses to Dehradun.

Best Time

April to end-June (till the arrival of the monsoon), and again from mid-September to mid-December (depending on the onset of winter snows). The Manju Kanta Pass could still have lots of snow till the end of May.

Altitude

Netwar is only at 4,578 ft / 1,380 m). The high campsites are at Ruinsara Tal at 11,000 ft / 3,350 m) and the ridge camp of Dhara at 12,796 ft / 3,900 m. The Manju Kanta Pass is the highest point of the trek at 14,108 ft / 4,300 m.

Highlights

Beautiful high altitude lake of Ruinsara Tal with great mountain views; spectacular meadows at Har Ki Dun; beautiful villages of the Tons valley; a visit to the pilgrimage centre of Yamnotri to purify your sins!

Support Services

Porters can be hired from Netwar, the road head, but most of them come from the villages of Taluka and Osla further up the valley. Schedule some time for these arrangements. Or drive further up the valley to Sankri or Taluka if the road conditions permit. Minimal food is available on the trail, so be self-equipped from Dehradun itself. Easy-to-follow trails and basic guest houses at Netwar, Seema and Har Ki Dun valley, but a guide must show the way to Manju Kanta Pass. Guides can be hired at Osla in advance.

Emergency

Basic medical facilities on the trail at Yamnotri only.
Rescue services available but difficult to arrange; telephones in larger villages.

■ Wild daffodils

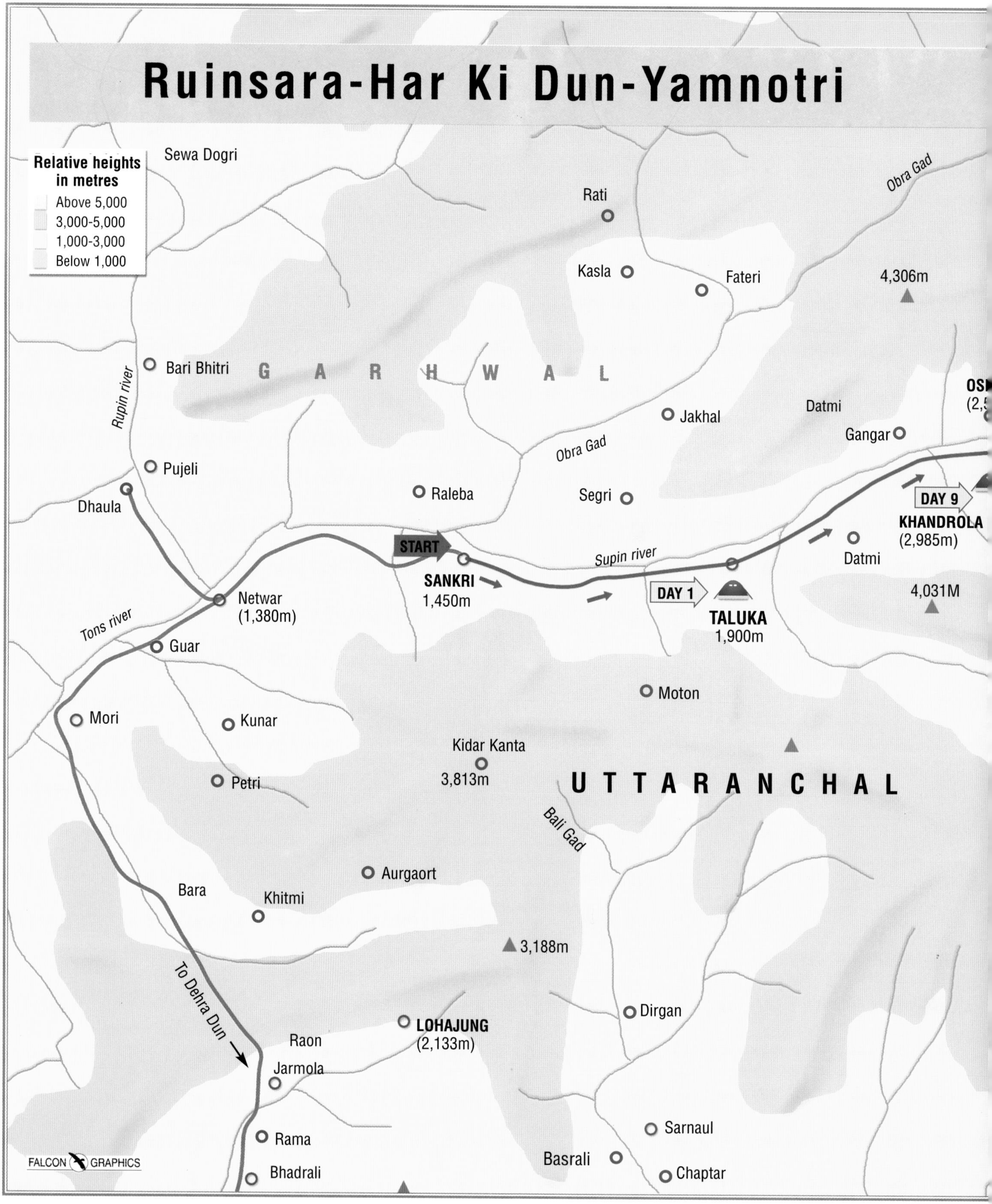

Ruinsara-Har Ki Dun-Yamnotri

Relative heights in metres
- Above 5,000
- 3,000-5,000
- 1,000-3,000
- Below 1,000

Sewa Dogri

Rati

Kasla

Fateri

4,306m

Obra Gad

G A R H W A L

Bari Bhitri

Rupin river

Datmi

OSI (2,5

Jakhal

Gangar

Pujeli

Obra Gad

Segri

DAY 9
KHANDROLA
(2,985m)

Dhaula

Raleba

Datmi

START

Supin river

DAY 1

Netwar
(1,380m)

SANKRI
1,450m

TALUKA
1,900m

4,031M

Tons river

Guar

Moton

Mori

Kunar

Kidar Kanta
3,813m

U T T A R A N C H A L

Petri

Bali Gad

Bara

Aurgaort

Khitmi

▲ 3,188m

To Dehra Dun

Dirgan

LOHAJUNG
(2,133m)

Raon

Jarmola

Rama

Sarnaul

Bhadrali

Basrali

Chaptar

FALCON GRAPHICS

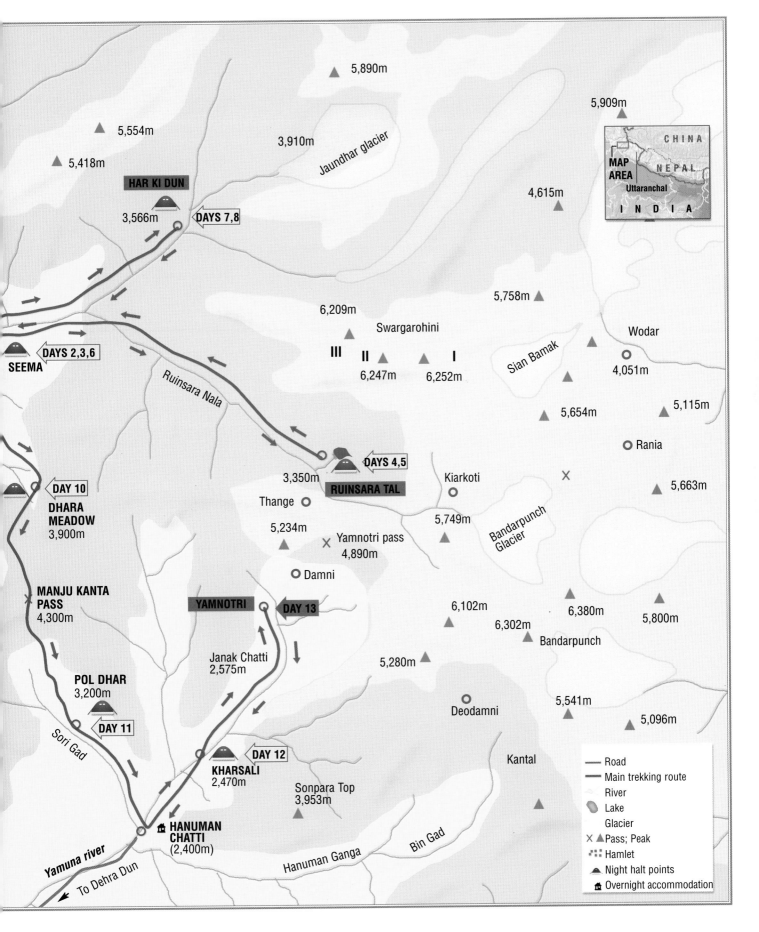

5,890m

5,554m

5,418m

3,910m

Jaundhar glacier

5,909m

CHINA

MAP AREA

NEPAL

Uttaranchal

I N D I A

4,615m

HAR KI DUN

3,566m

DAYS 7,8

5,758m

6,209m

Swargarohini

Wodar

III   II   I

6,247m   6,252m

Sian Bamak

4,051m

DAYS 2,3,6

SEEMA

Ruinsara Nala

5,654m

5,115m

Rania

5,663m

3,350m

DAYS 4,5

RUINSARA TAL

Kiarkoti

DAY 10

DHARA MEADOW
3,900m

Thange

5,749m

Bandarpunch Glacier

5,234m

Yamnotri pass
4,890m

MANJU KANTA PASS
4,300m

Damni

6,102m

6,380m

5,800m

YAMNOTRI

DAY 13

6,302m

Bandarpunch

POL DHAR
3,200m

Janak Chatti
2,575m

5,280m

DAY 11

5,541m

Deodamni

5,096m

Sori Gad

DAY 12

KHARSALI
2,470m

Kantal

Road

Main trekking route

River

Lake

Glacier

Sonpara Top
3,953m

Pass; Peak

Hamlet

HANUMAN CHATTI
(2,400m)

Night halt points

Overnight accommodation

Yamuna river

To Dehra Dun

Hanuman Ganga

Bin Gad

I Ruinsara Tal at 11,000 ft / 3,350 m at the base of Swargarohini Peak

Sustained logging has had its effect. Though this place was designated a sanctuary in the 1950s, forestry operations continue. Consequently, soil erosion has led to minor landslides.

I **DAY 2**: A steep one-hour hike brings you to Datmi village, where the view opens up to the upper valley of the Supin river. From there the trail climbs up slowly on a rocky, staircase-like path through lush pine and deodar forests to reach just below Gangar village, across the bridge. Another steady two-hour walk takes you to Seema (8,320 ft / 2,536 m), a cluster of tea shops and buildings next to a forest rest house. Camp next to the river or stay at the rest house.

I **DAY 3**: Osla village is perched above Seema across the Supin, and you can explore the village and fix a guide for the climb up to the Manju Kanta Pass. The rest of the time could be spent birdwatching.

I **DAY 4**: The trail to Ruinsara Tal goes past the river bridge to cross a side stream, and then climbs up steeply to reach a meadow where Gujjar shepherds camp in the summer. The Kala Nag range is visible with views of the Bandarpunch and Kala Nag peaks. A short descent brings you to the Ruinsara Nala. Cross the stream and climb up steadily, first through pine and deodar forests and then through rhododendron and birch to reach the serene blue waters of Ruinsara Tal (11,000 ft / 3,350 m).

I **DAYS 5-6**: Spend the day exploring the area around the lake which is situated just below the south face of Swargarohini and Bandarpunch II & III. The day after, retrace your steps to Seema on your way to Har Ki Dun.

DAYS 7-8: Cross the bridge on Supin to its right bank. The trail climbs for half an hour followed by a steep gradient for the next hour or so. You are walking with the river on your right and forests on your left. Climbing slowly for three hours you reach the huge rolling meadows of Har Ki Dun (11,700 ft / 3,566 m). The rest house is on one side of the meadow, surrounded by huge boulders and birch trees with a view of the grasslands in front. You could either stay in the rest house or camp outside on the meadow. With the west face of Swargarohini keeping vigil over the amphitheatre, Har Ki Dun is one of the prettiest spots in the Garhwal Himalaya. According to a legend from Mahabharata, Yudhishtir, the eldest of the Pandava princes, ascended onto heaven at the end of the great war, after reaching the top of the needle-shaped Swargarohini. One look at the summit would leave you with no doubt that it could indeed lead nowhere but to holy heaven. A good trekking option is the climb to Burasu Pass that leads to the Baspa valley in Kinnaur.

DAY 9: Return to Seema. Climb up from the lumber mill next to a side stream, just a short walk away from the rest house. There is no well-defined trail, so take a guide. A straight four-hour climb brings you to the Gujjar settlement of Khandrola (9,794 ft / 2,985 m). The camp is set in a clearing surrounded by spruce trees.

DAY 10: A steep one-hour climb from Khandrola leads to a hump leading on to rolling meadows. The trail traverses the mountainside for two and a half hours to the left, goes through a rich rhododendron forest, and then descends to a stream. Crossing over, the trail climbs up forty-five minutes to reach another stream and then ascends to the small ridge of Dhara (12,796 ft / 3,900 m). The campsite is in a meadow next to a lake with Gujjar huts close by.

DAY 11: The trail climbs up the grassy ridge above the camp. A short scramble on a rock face on the ridge and a walk along its exposed face brings you to a lateral moraine. The trail crosses the moraine and climbs on to another grassy ridge to ascend to the snowline, keeping to the left. Another scramble and you are atop the Manju Kanta Pass marked by a number of cairns. You get a typical high-altitude Garhwal view: The Kala Nag complex just above you and the Gangotri peaks behind them; Shrikanth and Jaonli Peaks to the north-east; and the snow-capped mountains of Kinnaur to your north. Plummeting below is the rather ill-defined trail to the Yamuna valley. Descending steeply on an exposed mountainside and then on a scree slope, reach camp at Pol Dhar (10,500 ft / 3,200 m) near the Sori Gad stream.

DAY 12: Climb up from the camp to the ridge on the left and then descend steeply through a dense forest for four hours to reach Banas. The trail crosses the bridge over Yamuna to meet the pilgrim route to Yamnotri, coming up from Hanuman Chatti. A slow climb of another hour and a half brings you to Kharsali (8,104 ft / 2,470 m).

DAY 13: Start early for the temple at Yamnotri and the holy hot springs. The setting there is dramatic with a waterfall forming the backdrop of the temple. From Yamnotri reach Hanuman Chatti in five hours and catch a bus back to the plains.

I Brahmini duck (*Ruddy Shellduck*)

■I Sunset from Sangor Meadow below Kaliheni Pass; the finger-like peak in the middle is Indra Killa

6

Holy Himachal

'In a hundred ages of the gods I could not tell thee the glories of Himachal. As the dew is dried up by the morning sun, so are the sins of mankind by the sight of Himachal.'

THESE oft-quoted lines from *Skanda Purana*, a Vedic text, were written with the entire Himalaya in mind. But the words are apt in either case. As a microcosm of all that the Himalaya have to offer, this remarkable state is a precious little necklace studded with jewels. Complicated lives can be altered by the experience of Himachal and its touch can restore sanity.

Myth and history have always coalesced in Himachal and historical truth has had to be extracted from enchanting legend. The first evidence of human civilisation in Himachal came in the shape of palaeolithic tools in Kangra and Guler. Almost 40,000 years old, these tools resembled those found in the Sohan valley, Pakistan.

Himachal's history took a major turn around 3,000-2,500 B.C. when the Aryans crossed the Ravi as part of their northward expansion. Early forms of democracy took shape thanks to the interaction between tribes. But since there was no single political authority, Himachal was dotted with republics. Invaders and empire builders meant that these small states could not but acknowledge the ruler's supremacy. In the early nineteenth century, fearing a Gorkha takeover,

the rajas of Himachal asked the British, who never ignored possible chances of expansion, for help. After the suppression of the Gorkhas, the British took direct control of the areas around what was to be known as Shimla. With time, the hill states also came under their suzerainty.

Himachal Pradesh is also of strategic importance because of its border with Tibet in the east. To the north are the Ladakh, Zanskar, Kishtwar and Jammu regions of Jammu & Kashmir. Punjab lies to its west and Haryana to the south. To the south-east, it shares a border with Uttar Pradesh. The lower hills of the Shivalik range roll into the plains in the south of the state, whereas the perennial snows on Pir Panjal, Zanskar, Dhunladhar, and the great Himalayan ranges feed Himachal's great chain of rivers.

The enchanting valleys of Chamba, Kangra, Kulu, Kinnaur, Lahaul and Spiti have developed unique cultural identities. The rituals and beliefs of the people who have settled in Himachal make for a terrific package. The nomadic Gaddis of Bhramaur, the warlike Dogras of Chamba, the industrious Lahaulis, the friendly Spitians, the charming Kinnaurs, and the merry inhabitants of Kulu and Kangra, all have their special characteristics. With the establishment of the Tibetan Government-in-Exile at Dharamsala, a new ethnic group has become a part of Himachal.

It's the abundant beauty of Himachal that gives its people their character of simplicity and modesty. Due to its varied climatic conditions and altitudes, the state can be divided into three regions: The Trans-Himalaya, of the cold deserts of Lahaul, Spiti, and Kinnaur; the Himalaya, which is subdivided into the high and middle mountains; and the semi-arid zone consisting of the Shivalik foothills. Nearly one-third of Himachal is under forest cover and almost one-fifth or twenty per cent of the state is covered by national parks and sanctuaries. With thirty-one such areas, Himachal Pradesh has the second largest number of national parks and sanctuaries in the country.

■I Columbines

■I A high-altitude meadow in upper Spiti, near Kunjum La

Trek I

Spiti: Drive-cum-Trek

The children of Spiti in north-west Himachal get their first toys to play with from nature. These are fossilised molluscs and ammonites, precursors to the marine life in our oceans. Embedded in the bed of the Spiti river is evidence of the Tethys sea that existed at the place where the Himalaya stands today.

Spiti is far away from everywhere. Because of its proximity to Tibet, it existed behind the forbidden 'inner-line'. Now entry permits are available from Delhi, Shimla, and Kulu. The approach to Spiti, however, is restricted because of its isolation. Spiti lies between Ladakh, Tibet, Lahaul, Kulu, and Kinnaur. After Independence it became a part of Punjab and later, a district of Himachal Pradesh.

Spiti can be approached from the Kulu valley over the Rohtang Pass into Lahaul and then over the Kunjum Pass into the main valley. But these passes are snowbound most of the year. The main route goes on the Hindustan-Tibet highway, along the gorge of the Satluj. From Shimla, it takes two days to drive to Spiti, through Bushahr and Kinnaur. On the first two days after you enter Spiti, visit the monasteries at Tabo, Dhankhar, and Ki. You will get acclimatised, and acquainted with Spiti's heritage.

Situated thirty-five kilometres west of the confluence of Satluj and Spiti rivers, at Sumdo, the official entry point to Spiti, is the Tabo monastery. Driving forty kilometres to the west of Tabo, reach the spectacular setting of

Ways & Means

Duration

4 days of walking and 6 to 7 days of driving

Degree of Difficulty

2: Easy to moderate

Getting There

There are various options. Drive in from Manali or from Shimla. From Shimla, a two-day drive will lead you into the Spiti valley up to Tabo monastery. From Manali, a two-day drive will get you to Kaza. Spend a few days exploring the monasteries of Tabo, Dhankhar, and Ki before starting the trek.

Best Time

From Shimla, approach as early as mid-April and exit the Spiti valley as late as mid-November as there is no high pass to negotiate. From Manali, the Rohtang pass and the Kunjum La restrict the visit from about mid-June to early October, depending on the snow conditions on these passes.

Altitude

On the trek the highest point reached is the Yang La at 16,000 ft / 4,876 m and the highest campsite is at Demul at 14,700 ft / 4,480 m. If driving in from Manali, the highest point reached is the Kunjum La at 14, 932 ft / 4,551 m.

Highlights

The monasteries at Tabo, Dhankhar, and Ki on the drive, and the *gompas* at Komik on the trek. It is a high-altitude trek, yet an easy one since it is mostly over fossil-strewn trails. The trek has spectacular mountain vistas.

Support Services

Very few pack mules and horses available at Langja, the road head, so they must be arranged for in advance. Agents in Kaza can do this, but must be given some days to get to Langja. Must be totally self-equipped, no facilities on the trail. Food can be bought in Kaza but camping equipment is available only in Manali or Shimla.

Emergency

Manali and Shimla are the last stops for medical facilities. The Spiti valley is connected by phone but once on the trek, no medical or rescue facility is available.

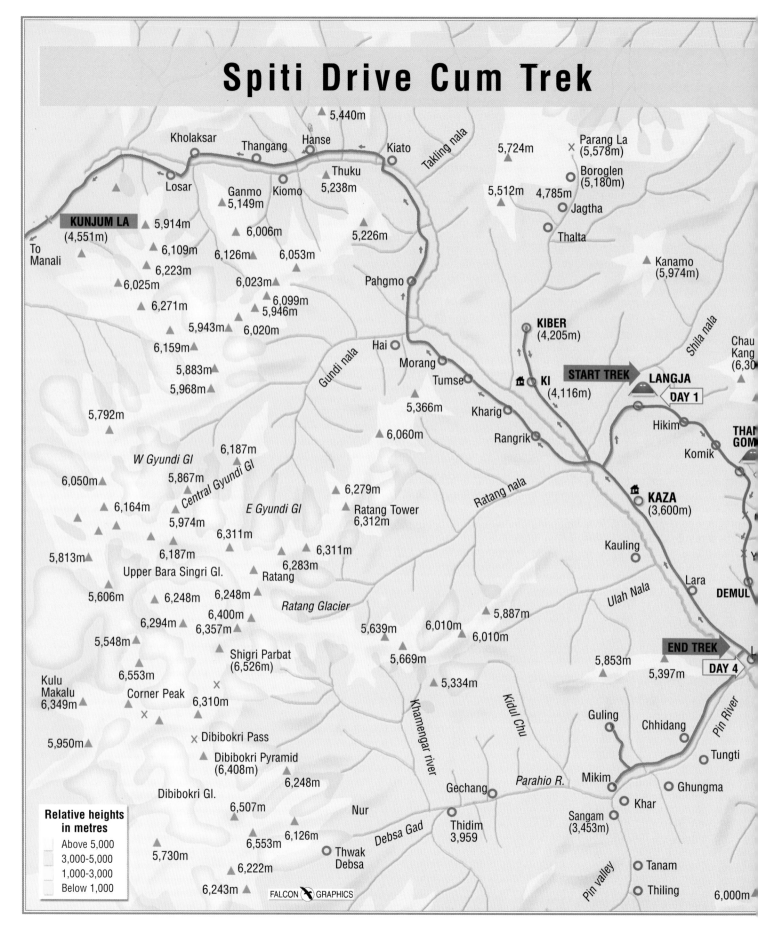

Spiti Drive Cum Trek

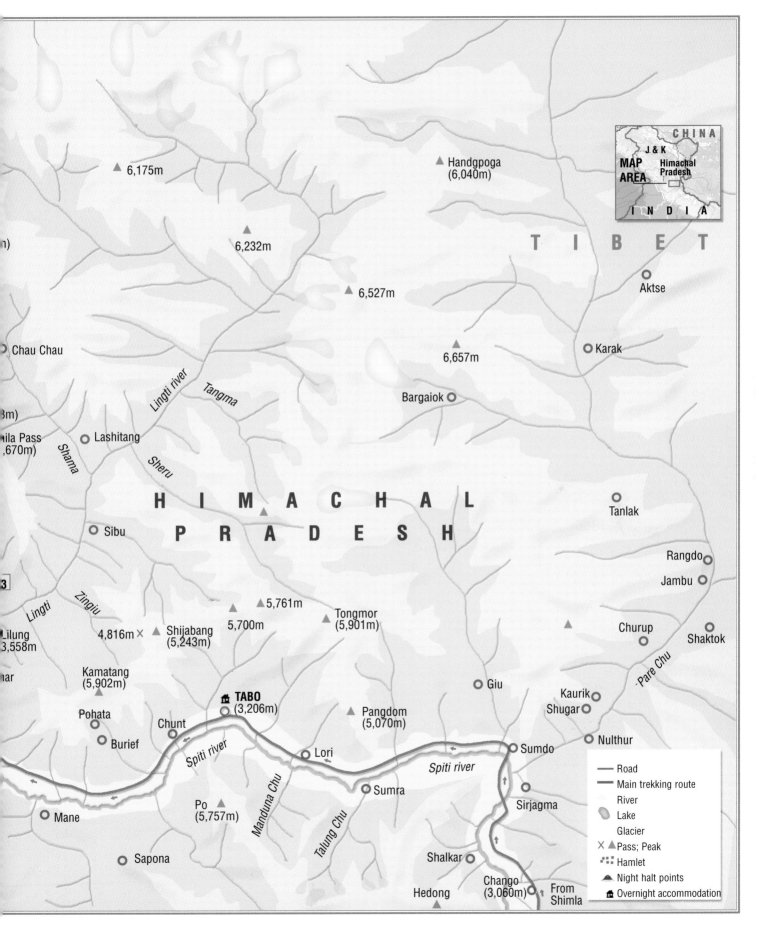

▌I The *gompa* at Ki. The Rinpoche here is the reincarnation of Rinchen Zangpo, also known as The Great Translator.

I The ridge-top *gompa* and Dhankhar village; below: Formations near the *gompa*

Dhankhar Gompa, the traditional capital of Spiti. A beautiful statue of the Buddha in meditation (Vairocana) is the highlight. The other attraction is a two and a half kilometre-hike to a high-altitude lake (13,500 ft / 4,115 m) that makes for a perfect camping site. Camp here or down in the valley on the Spiti river. Next day you could drive on to the Ki Gompa.

■| The Sakyapa Gompa of Thangyud near the village of Komik

The Ki monastery, the largest in Spiti, is an hour's drive from Kaza, the administrative headquarters. It was invaded umpteen times by the Mongols in the seventeenth century and then the Ladakhis, Dogras, and Sikhs in the nineteenth. Ki has a collection of sacred Buddhist paintings or *thangkas* said to be two hundred years old. There are frescoes on Guru Padmasambhava, a collection of old weapons, and a couple of three-metre-long trumpets.

■ **DAY 1**: After breakfast at Kaza, leave for the village of Langja, the road head. An hour's drive on a steep road leads to the village. Big vehicles find it difficult to negotiate this narrow road, so take a taxi from Kaza. Camp at Langja and go on a few walks to acclimatise. The village is situated on an undulating meadow at 14,500 ft / 4,419 m. In July, you can see the land being tilled by yaks for the barley crop. The hillside on the left rises towards the summits of Kanamo Peak (19,600 ft / 5,974 m) and the conical Chau Chau Kang Nilde (20,680 ft / 6,303 m). A perfect place to meditate.

■ **DAY 2**: The trail goes on through meadow country. All through the trek you would be parallel to the Spiti river, walking between 14,000 ft / 4,250 m and 16,000 ft / 4,900 m. Once acclimatised, this trek would turn out to be just a stroll through a majestic highland setting. After leaving the camp, a one-and-a-half hour climb would take you to a small saddle (15,000 ft / 4,572 m) from where you could take a forty-five-minute detour to the meadow's edge. Down below is Kaza town with the Spiti river. Across the valley, towards Kulu, is the Bara

■l Tabo village and *gompa*, spread out on a plain above the Spiti river

Singri Glacier, dominated by the Ratang Peak and Ratang Tower (both 20,700 ft / 6,310 m). Rejoin the main trail. A steady ninety-minute walk takes you to Hikkim village nestled in a bowl-shaped valley. In another hour, you reach Komik village just below the Thangyud monastery, next to which camp can be set.

Thangyud monastery belongs to the Sakya Pa sect of Tibetan Buddhism and was founded in 1071 A.D., as a result of a reformist movement. Taking its name from the yellow colour of the

The magic of Tabo

SENT to India by Yeshe Od, the King of Guge in western Tibet, to bring back the wisdom of Buddhism, Rinchen Zangpo translated 158 holy scriptures from Sanskrit into Tibetan. He is also credited with building 108 monasteries and stupas (monuments containing Buddha's relics). Tabo is not merely a monastery but a *chos khor*, a doctrinal enclave. Designed in western Tibetan style and painted by artisans brought from Kashmir by Zangpo, Tabo is a paradise of human creativity. The complex has nine temples, 23 *chortens*, and chambers for monks and nuns. The assembly hall or the *du-khang* contains frescoes depicting scenes from the life of the Buddha and stucco figures of gods and goddesses. The wall facing the main door is decorated with the thirteen-foot, seated figure of the four-faced Vairocana, the Buddha in meditation. The *lakhang* or the monks' main prayer hall has a large figure of Sakyamuni or Siddhartha Gautam seated in a diamond position with a bowl in his lap. There is also a *ser khang* or a golden temple with lovely paintings of Gandharvas (angels specialising in the arts), birds, and floral motifs. Tabo's 1000th anniversary celebrations in 1996 drew a large number of visitors from all over the world and His Holiness the Dalai Lama performed the *kalachakra* ceremony for world peace.

■I The top of the Kunjum La or pass at 14,932 ft / 4,551 m

soil (*sakya* is Tibetan for 'tawny earth') found near its first monastery in western Tibet, the sect provided some prominent Buddhist scholars. The monastery was built in the early fourteenth century on the pattern of a Chinese castle. It has massive slanted walls for defence against invaders. The Sakya Pa monastery at Kaza is of fairly recent origin. Exquisite statues of Maitreya and Guru Padmasambhava are the highlights at Thangyud.

■I **DAY 3**: Climb up from the Gompa for an hour to Chame La (15,350 ft / 4,678 m). Beyond this point are the meadows of Kuangme. In another two and a half hours you reach Yang La (16,000 ft / 4,876 m), the highest trek point. From there, descend to Demul at 14,700 ft / 4,480 m. In the evening, take a walk above the village to sight the handsome Himalayan wolf. An absolutely clear, star-studded sky could keep you busy till pretty late if you have any interest in star-gazing.

■I **DAY 4**: Walk through the village to the Dolma La (15,200 ft / 4,633 m) and reach the end of the plateau. Descend to the road head of Lidang (11,600 ft / 3,536 m). This is a slippery trail, so be careful. A vehicle should be waiting for you as there is no public or private transport available. Drive back to Kaza and then over Kunjum and Rohtang passes to Manali. Your brief encounter with Buddhism is over, may its salutary effect last forever. *Om Mane Padme Hum!*

Trek II

Manikaran-Pin Parbati Pass-Pin Valley

In the sylvan surroundings of the Manikaran region it is believed that Lord Shiva, angry at a domestic squabble, went off into the fields and there under the cool shade of a tall cannabis plant, he suddenly experienced comfort and bliss. He ate some of its leaves and, impressed, endorsed the plant. He came to be regarded as the Lord of *Bhang* (*bhang*: hashish or marijuana). Connoisseurs all over the world agree that Manikaran produces the best hashish in the world. But, surely, this is not the reason why you should be going on the Manikaran-Pin Parbati trek! Manikaran, famous for its medicinal hot springs, is a temple town built around a Gurdwara and a Hindu shrine. First, reach Bhuntar on the Kulu road by air or by road.

■I DAY 1: Leave early for Manikaran. Driving up the Parbati valley (named after Lord Shiva's consort), you reach the temple town in two hours. After spending time visiting the houses of worship, and arranging porters, leave for Pulga village, a four-and-a-half-hour walk from Manikaran. Leaving Manikaran, the trail ascends gradually on the right bank of Parbati for an hour to reach Rastar, a hamlet, after which the road ends. After another two hours, the trail crosses the river on a sturdy wooden bridge to traverse the mountainside. Crossing two side streams, climb steeply through oak forests and fields to reach the Pulga village (9,154 ft / 2,791 m). An old rest

Ways & Means

Duration
11 days

Degree of Difficulty
4 to 5: Moderate to rigorous, rigorous

Getting There
In the tourist season there could be several flights a day to Bhunter airport, a two-hour drive from Manali. From Bhunter, a side valley leads to the town of Manikaran, a two-to-three-hour drive. There is no need to go to Manali. Drive further from Manikaran over a rough road to across the valley from Pulga, an hour's effort. It is an hour's walk to cross the valley to reach Pulga village. Or, the drive up from the plains begins at Chandigarh, which takes up to eleven to twelve hours to Manikaran, via Bhunter.

Best Time
May (snow conditions permitting) to early July and again from September to end-November (or later if there is no fresh snow over the Pin-Parbati Pass). The Dussehra festival in Kulu in October is worth attending.

Altitude
Manikaran at 5,600 ft / 1,707 m is the starting point and the highest altitude is at Pin-Parbati Pass, 17,452 ft / 5,319 m. The highest camp is at 15,150 ft / 4,617 m.

Highlights
The Parbati valley with lush meadows full of wild flowers and waterfalls and scenic campsites; the hot springs at Khir Ganga. The spectacular crossing of the glaciated pass has excellent views, from the green Parbati valley to the stark Pin valley. There is an opportunity to visit monasteries in Spiti valley.

Support Services
Only porters can cross the Pin-Parbati Pass and these are available in Manikaran and in Pulga. Other camping services are available only in Manali, but there are trek organisers and basic rations in Manikaran and Pulga too. Some good guest houses in Manikaran and Pulga and some very basic ones in Khir Ganga, at the hot spring, offering food. For the rest of the trek, one must be self-equipped.

Emergency
Manali or Bhunter is the only place to get medical help or rescue facilities. In Spiti, phone links are available.

■I *Impatiens sulcata* from the Balsam family

Manikaran-Pin Parbati Pass-Pin Valley

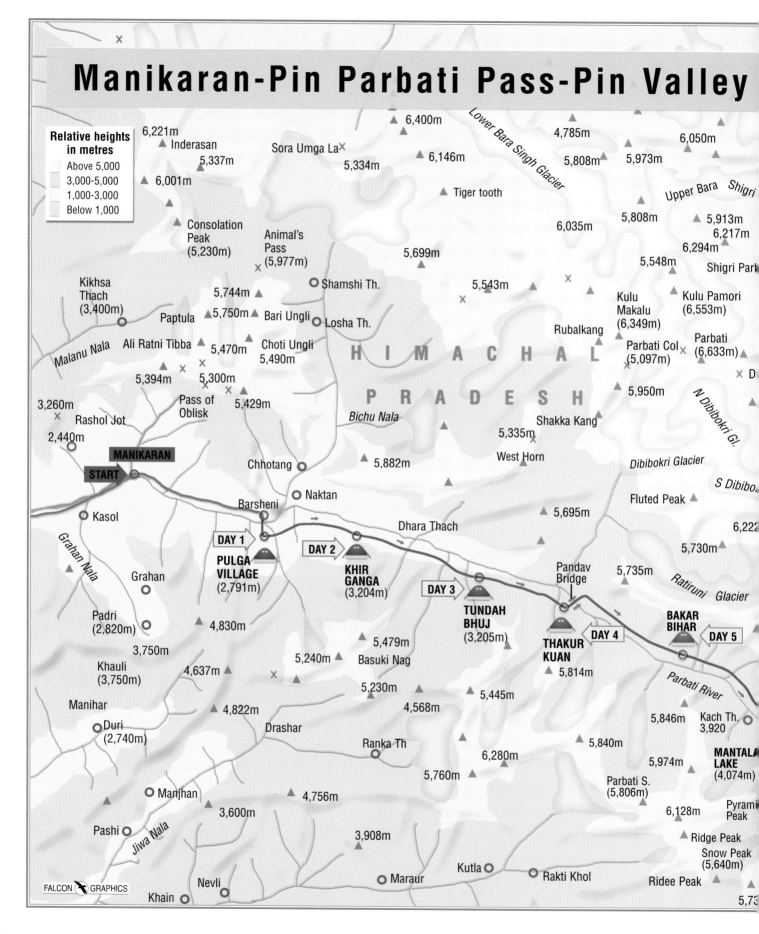

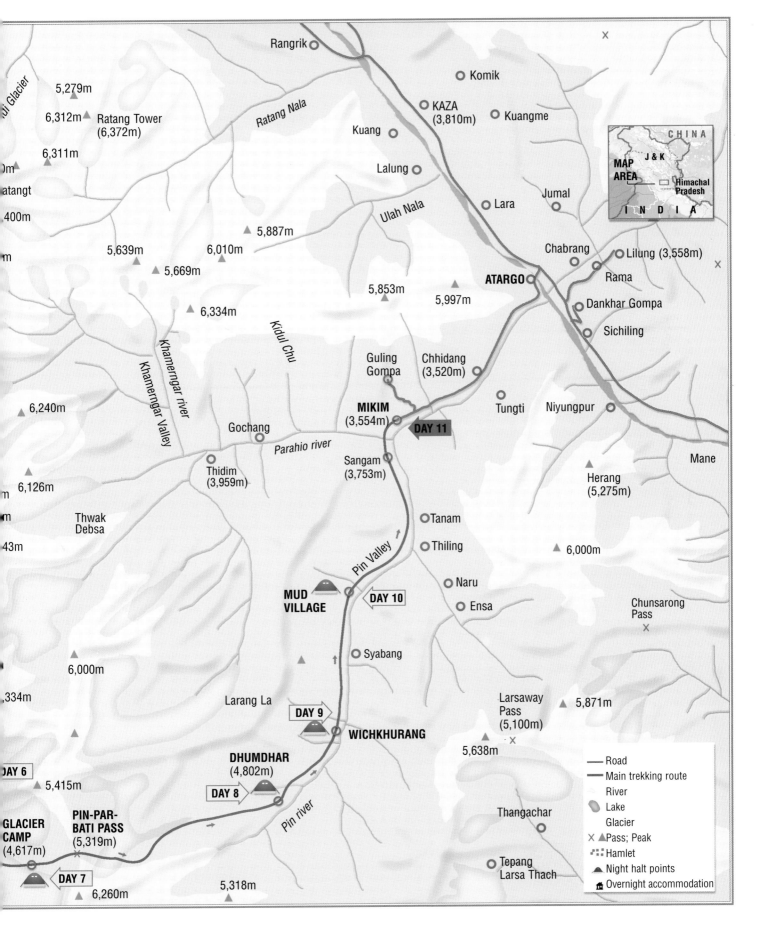

■I The village deity or *gram devata* at the festival in Pulga village, Parbati valley

house in the classical British mould is an invitation for the night. Later, in the evening, go down to the exquisitely carved village temple that does not have a deity. Almost three decades ago, the statue was forcibly stolen by the people of a village from the adjoining Jiva Nala valley. Since then, they have been generous enough to return it to Pulga for a festival only once.

■I **DAY 2**: Descend through the village and traverse the mountain for ninety minutes. The valley narrows down and the trail goes through a dense forest to lead to a river crossing via a high bridge. Moving up the right bank after a ten-minute climb, the trail crosses the torrential Tos Nala joining the Parbati river. After a thirty-minute traverse you reach Nakthena, the last village on the route. Walking through fields of *hashish* you reach Rudranag, an open patch in the forest overlooking a pretty waterfall. Under an overhang, there is a small shrine of Lord Shiva. Immediately after Rudranag, the trail crosses the Parbati back to the left bank over another stunning bridge, with a waterfall plunging into the river. A steady ascent with some steep stretches takes you to Khir Ganga (10,512 ft / 3,204 m). The trail moves through a primeval setting under a thick forest. As you climb higher, birch trees emerge and in two hours from Rudranag, you reach the campsite in the forest. The hot springs of Khir Ganga are a fifteen-minute walk up. Recommended.

■I **DAY 3**: The trail stays on the left bank all day. Crossing three side streams (the second one on precariously placed logs), it moves through a forest of rhododendrons, fir and birch for the first hour. Then you reach open pastures. After the third bridge, a forty-five-minute walk leads to the campsite at Tundah Bhuj (10,516 ft / 3,205 m) on a steep-sided meadow. Watch seven waterfalls cascading down from shiny black rocks across the valley (numbers could vary, but just after the monsoon, you will definitely see a lot of them). The impressive summit of the Kulu Eiger looms up at the valley end.

▐ **DAY 4**: After camp at Tundah Bhuj, the trail becomes tricky as it descends via a narrow and slippery path to the valley floor. You climb on to a cliff using your hands for support. On a ten-feet exposed stretch you have to perform regular rock climbing manoeuvres as you grope for footholds. It takes almost an hour. But, nature rewards you again as the valley opens up and the trail approaches a meadow bedecked with wild flowers. Almost prancing through the meadow for an hour, reach the campsite at Thakur Kuan (19,076 ft / 5,814 m) at a bend in the valley. Overlooking the camp, the Dibi Bokri river dashes out through a narrow gorge; Kulu Eiger keeps soaring triumphantly towards the sky and, for the first time, you catch the Parbati in a serene mood as it meanders past the campsite. Heaven on earth? Well, almost!

▐ **DAY 5**: Reach Pandav Pul in two hours. Climb over huge boulders on which a stone staircase has been cut out to cross a side stream. Then you clamber over another rock under which the Parbati has cut its way through. Sauntering through more meadows, you reach the Oriage Thach. The campsite is two hundred feet above the river on the Bakar Bihar Thach (12,517 ft / 3,815 m).

▐ **DAY 6**: A gentle walk on flat ground, then a stream you have to cross by hopping over boulders, and you are standing just below the towering massif of Kulu Eiger. The trail continues its moderate climb staying close to the soft flow of the Parbati, going past a few shepherd encampments. An hour-long ascent takes you away from the Gaddi shepherds to climb over the debris of a moraine descending from a side glacier to finally reach the Mantalai Lake (13,367 ft / 4,074 m). The lake has been formed by the natural dam created by the glacial moraine. Walking around the lake for half an hour, you reach the campsite on a grassy patch. Makeshift Lord Shiva shrines with tridents sticking out of rocks piled together are scattered around this sombre glaciated theatre. Desolate scree slopes, formidable rock formations and cold and reticent vistas of ice and snow will be your company for tonight — it's best to retire to bed early and wait for the sun to rise.

▐ **DAY 7**: There are no soft options open on the trek. Three formidable-looking gulleys situated on the left of the camp stare you in the face. The trail climbs up on the third and after a steady climb of three hours, past small ice pools, you reach a steep rocky patch with large sections of snow. Keeping to the right, continue climbing to a ridge top plateau (15,150 ft / 4,617 m), where you pitch camp just below the snout of a small glacier. Get a good view of the summits of Parbati South (19,049 ft / 5,806 m), Pyramid (20,105 ft / 6,128 m), and Ridge Peak (19,000 ft / 5,790 m).

Shimla in the Raj

CAPTAIN Kennedy, the first British Superintendent of the Hill States, was among the first to build a home for himself in the hills in 1821. Slowly, the salubrious climate drew a large number of British officers and their families in summer. A charming English conclave started developing in Shimla with clubs, pubs, and theatres. In 1864, Shimla became the summer capital of the empire. With the invention of railways, the British engineers blasted a rail road all the way up from Kalka to Shimla in 1903. The families lived in residences such as Sterling Castle and Barnes Court; travellers stayed at Lowrie's Hotel; polo was played at Annendale, and entertainment was provided at Gaiety theatre. As Emily Eden, the sister of Governor-General George Eden, wrote in her memoirs: 'Like meat, we keep better here. The sharp air is perfectly exhilarating. I have felt nothing like it — I mean nothing so English since I was on the terrace at East Combe.' Nostalgia and colonialism worked in tandem as Goddess Shyamala watched helplessly from her hill-top home on Jakhu Hill.

I Barley fields in Mud village, Pin valley, Spiti

DAY 8: Start early and climb for an hour over a steep moraine. Keeping to the glacier's left, reach a flat plateau with a dramatic hanging glacier in front. The trail climbs between the glacier and a rock face for another hour to take you to a snow field with a gradual incline. Veer slightly to the left of this heavily crevassed snow field to reach its high point. The pass is now visible to your left, though still some distance away. A steady climb for the next two hours takes you to its top (17,457 ft / 5,319 m). First, glimpse the Pin valley in Spiti; views also open up towards Kinnaur on your east with Kinner Kailash and Srikanth Mahadev on the horizon. To your north-west is the Bara Singri complex. Descend on a snow slope to cross a small stream. Following it steeply down for another two hours on its left bank, you reach the campsite of Dhumdhar (15,765 ft / 4,802 m) at the confluence of the Pin with a side stream.

DAY 9: A short climb on the side-stream's glacier is necessary because there is no place to cross it near the camp. Follow the main river down after crossing to the valley below. The trail joins the path coming down from the Tari Khango or Bhabha Pass that leads to Rampur Bushahr. Another forty-five minutes beyond this confluence take you to the Wichkhurang (12,600 ft / 3,840 m) campsite.

A large part of the Pin valley has been declared a national park. It supports a large population of ibex and blue sheep. The rare Tibetan gazelle and woolly hare are found there. Among the predators, the snow leopard and the Himalayan wolf are present, but extremely hard to sight.

DAY 10: The trail descends steadily on typical rock and rubble till it reaches a big cairn. Thereafter, the situation improves, and a gentle descent takes you to a side stream. You wade across and the steep-sided valley starts widening. The mountain scenery around you is hallucinatingly coloured: there are green, purple, and maroon hills. In another hour and a half, Mud village comes into view. The campsite is just outside the village and a fifteen-minute walk takes you to the local monastery on the hill side, gaily painted in red.

DAY 11: Cross the village down to the Pin river and follow its left bank till you reach a ledge on a cliff after two hours. Sangam and Mikim villages can be seen. Walking next to the ledge for an hour, past Sangam, reach Parahio Nala. Crossing this river on a pulley and then walking for another twenty minutes, you reach the campsite of Mikim, the end of the trek. The Guling Gompa, the oldest in Spiti, is an hour's walk away and worth a visit.

Drive to the confluence of Pin with Spiti. After crossing Atargo bridge across Spiti, you can take the left turn to go to Manali via Kaza and Kunjum and Rohtang passes, or turn right to go to Shimla via Kinnaur and Bushahr. You also have the option of sitting down on a roadside tea shop and wondering why treks have to end at all.

Trek III

Beas Kund-Bhrigu Lake

Ways & Means

Duration
6 days to cover both the lakes

Degree of Difficulty
2: Easy to moderate

Getting There
Manali is linked to Delhi by a flight. In the tourist season there are several a day coming into the airport at Bhunter, a two-hour drive from Manali. Book well in advance. Or drive up from the plains at Chandigarh for ten hours.

Best Time
April to June and from mid-September to early December. In October, Kulu celebrates Dussehra in a unique way.

Altitude
The Bhrigu lake is the highest point at 14,010 ft / 4,270 m). The last day is a hard descent of 7,000 ft / 2,134 m.

Highlights
The lakes of Beas Kund and Bhrigu; superb mountains views from Bhrigu.

Support Services
Many trek organisers in Manali make all the arrangements. On the Beas Kund stretch, there are *dhabas* and the trail is easy to find. Only carry your own tent for sleeping. On the Bhrigu section, be self-equipped and take a guide.

Emergency
Manali is the only place to provide medical help on this trip, but you are never far from it.

In the Vedic period, the upper catchment area of Beas river in the Kulu valley was called Kulantapith (End of the Habitable World) in Sanskrit. Stand at the top of the Rohtang Pass at the head of the valley to find out how appropriate this name is. Behind you lies the verdant Kulu valley, showered upon by monsoon clouds every year and irrigated by countless streams. In front of you is the rain-shadow area of Lahaul, desolate and stark. Not surprising then that the Indo-Aryans who settled in this valley didn't think much of the land beyond Rohtang. But for a trekker, some trails around this region are a must, the Beas Kund-Bhrigu lake trek being just one of them.

All Kulu valley treks are approachable from Kulu or Manali. The road from Manali crosses over the Beas and goes to the Rohtang Pass and then beyond to the Lahaul valley and Ladakh. A short way up this road is Palchan, a typical hill village, from where a turn-off takes you to Solang (fourteen kilometres from Manali), an alpine pasture. The meadows there transform into great ski slopes during the winters. February and March are the best months to ski. There are two and a half kilometres of runs served by a 300 m-ski lift.

■ **DAY 1**: The trail is on a Jeep track through dense deodars. A well-defined trail takes over from the track and a climb over grassy slopes followed by loose boulders brings you to the large alpine meadow of Dhundi, (9,310 ft / 2,840 m). Dhundi is an excellent habitat for pheasants like monals and koklas. From the campsite, the north face of Hanuman Tibba (19,813 ft / 6,039 m) can be seen.

■ **DAY 2**: Cross a snow bridge over the Beas and get on to a loose scree slope. You reach a ridge over which the river forms a waterfall and then go on to Lualli. Climbing the ridge beyond this place, you descend to a huge valley with the pea-shaped Beas Kund on the left. The summits of Hanuman Tibba, Shitidhar (17,370 ft / 5,294 m), Ladakhi, Manali, Friendship and Kulu Peaks surround the lake in a semi-circle – a memorable sight.

■ **DAY 3**: Walk back to Solang and drive to Palchan. A trail criss-crossing the metal road leads to Kothi (8,497 ft / 2,590 m). Stay at the forest rest house or camp in the grounds around where pine forests hold sway. Due to its location, Kothi tends to get pretty windy and cold in the evenings.

■ **DAY 4**: A steep five-hour climb on a shepherd's trail takes you to Moridhung (12,000 ft / 3,657 m), a meadow beyond the tree-line. Take a guide along as a maze of trails cuts across the main route. On the way up, the road to Rohtang (12,400 ft / 3,780 m) wends to the north. The summits of Mukar Beh (19,750 ft / 6,020 m) and Shikar Beh (20,000 ft / 6,096 m) lie behind to the west.

▮I Pilgrims from Vashisht village at Bhrigu Lake

▮I DAY 5: Climb to Bhrigu (14,010 ft / 4,270 m), a lake whose shining emerald green waters stand out against the rocky ridge surrounding it. Circumnavigate the lake and climb on to the ridge. An easy scramble takes you to the top (14,400 ft / 4,389 m). Hanuman Tibba is to your west, and the Mulkila (21,400 ft / 6,522 m) and Chandrabhaga peaks lie to the north in Lahaul. To the south-east are the razor sharp summits of Indrakila, Deo Tibba (19,700 ft / 6,004 m) and Indrasen (20,500 ft / 6,248 m). You also get a scary view of the Hamta valley on the other side of the ridge. Retrace your steps to the lake. In August a thick carpet of flowers covers the meadows around – gentians, columbines, edelweiss, potentillas, and anemones. Spend a day exploring the meadows around the lake.

▮I DAY 6: On the last day, the steep trail switchbacks through a thick pine forest to take you to Vashisht, a village above Manali. Tired after this (2,134 ft / 7,000 m) descent, plunge into the hot water springs there, and then climb down to the river and walk across the bridge to Manali, or take a taxi back to Manali.

The enclosed map marks out an additional route on which you can walk from Manali itself along the right bank of the river via the village of Goshal. It takes a whole day to cover the distance from Manali to Solang. Also, to save on the steep climb to Moridhung one could take a taxi from Palchan to Gulaba on the road to Rohtang and climb the hill from there to Moridhung. This route is also shown in the map.

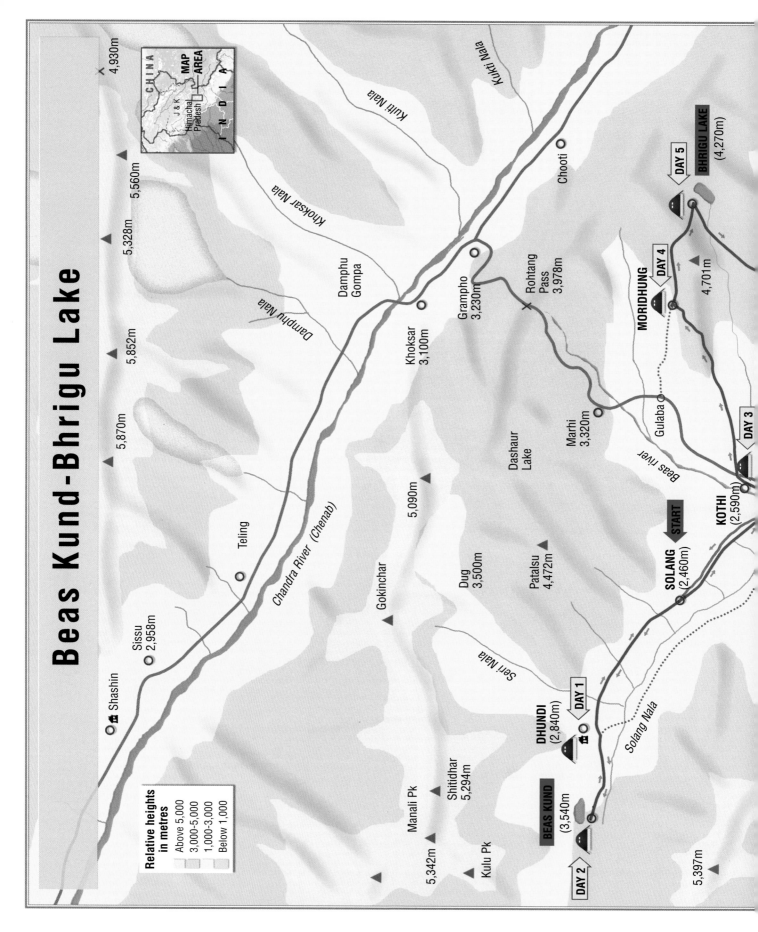

Beas Kund-Bhrigu Lake

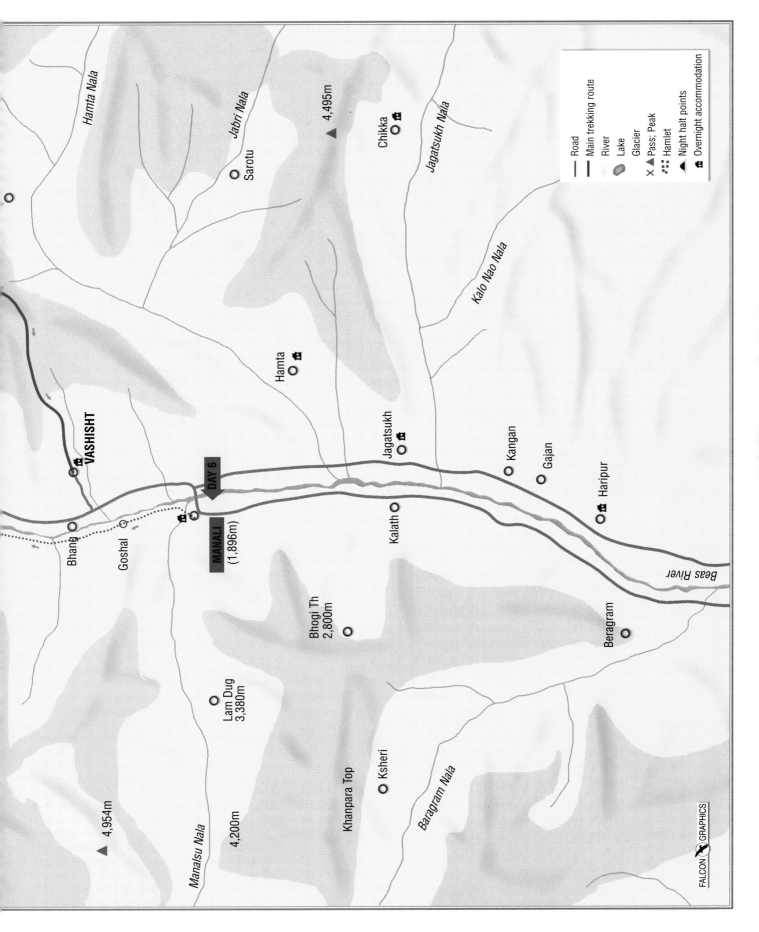

Trek IV

Tirthan Valley

Himachal Pradesh has taken the lead in advocating and implementing environmental conservation. The Great Himalayan National Park situated in the eastern catchment area of the Beas is a biologically rich terrain that is complemented by scenery. The Tirthan which, along with Sainj and Jiwa rivers, flows westward to feed the Beas, falls within the national park. For a naturalist as well as the trekker, the river valley is full of possibilities.

The Tirthan river valley has always been a popular hunting ground as it abounds with big game. Due to the threat of hunting, Tirthan was notified as a sanctuary in 1976, much before the idea of the Great Himalayan National Park was floated.

Reaching Kulu valley by air or road, take official permission to enter the National Park from its headquarters at Shamshi, down the road from the airport at Bhuntar. If possible make a brief stop at the Sai Ropa forest rest house to get the latest route information.

■I **DAY 1**: Starting early from Kulu, backtrack to a hamlet perched over the Beas. Taking the diversion to Larji, follow the Tirthan river to Gushaini. A little temple in Gushaini is dedicated to Garga Durga, the local deity. A system of three-fold worship has been practised in Himachal since the time of the Khasas: there is an *ishta devata* (the personal deity), a *kul devata* (the family deity), and a *gram devata* (the village deity). Most deities

Ways & Means

Duration

9 days

Degree of Difficulty

3: Moderate

Permits

The trek is in the Great Himalayan National Park and needs the permission of the wildlife warden based at Shamshi, near Bhunter – the airport in Kulu valley.

Getting There

A flight links Bhunter airport with Delhi. There are daily flights in a small plane during the tourist season, but book well in advance. It takes about three hours of driving to reach Gushaini, the road head, from Bhunter. Alternatively, the drive up from the plains begins at Chandigarh and takes ten to eleven hours to get to Gushaini.

Best Time

April to June and again from mid-September to early December. Sometime in October is the Dussehra festival, which is celebrated in Kulu in a unique way and is worth a visit.

Altitude

Gushaini is at 5,100 ft / 1,554 m. Highest campsite is at Bhiundwari at 12,000 ft / 3,657 m.

Highlights

High altitude meadows full of wild flowers in the spring and summer; thick virgin forests well endowed with plants and animals; very rarely visited by other trekkers.

Support Services

Porters are available at Gushaini village but it takes time to arrange for them. Must be self equipped for all camping and food; no facilities on the route.

Emergency

Kulu is the only place to provide medical help and rescue facilities. There are no villages, so no help can be expected once on the trail.

■I The monal pheasant

were human beings who acquired merit due to a great deed or sacrifice. Leaving the temple behind at Gushaini (5,100 ft / 1,554 m), climb the trail to Kharaungcha (6,700 ft / 2,042 m), the entry to the National Park. A steep climb along the Tirthan, with many side trails leading on to the villages around, brings you to Kharaungcha, where you can stay at a forest rest house or pitch a tent. The Gushaini villagers make good guides.

■❙ **DAY 2**: A gradual descent from Kharaungcha takes you to the river bank. Short of the guard hut at Rolla, cross over to the right bank. From there, the valley narrows down and the Tirthan thunders near by. Trees on either side of the bank form an arch as you make your way through dense vegetation. This is prime pheasant country and is also regarded as one of the last refuges of the rare western tragopan. With a scarlet plumage and white spottings on the feathers, it is a handsome bird. After two hours of walking from Rolla through the dense forest, reach the guard hut at Chalocha. The gorge is so narrow, you sometimes have to climb up on step ladders cut out from tree trunks. From Chalocha, unrelenting switchbacks take you to Jathor, a flat clearing in the forest. Climb onto the saddle on the ridge above to descend to the wild meadow of Nara (10,700 ft / 3,261 m). Camping on this meadow below the ridge you can see the summit of Srikand Mahadev.

■❙ **DAY 3**: The meadows there are the ideal habitat for the Himalayan tahr. Regarded as an intermediate between a goat-antelope and goat, it is a well-

■❙ Nara Thach (meadow) in the Tirthan valley

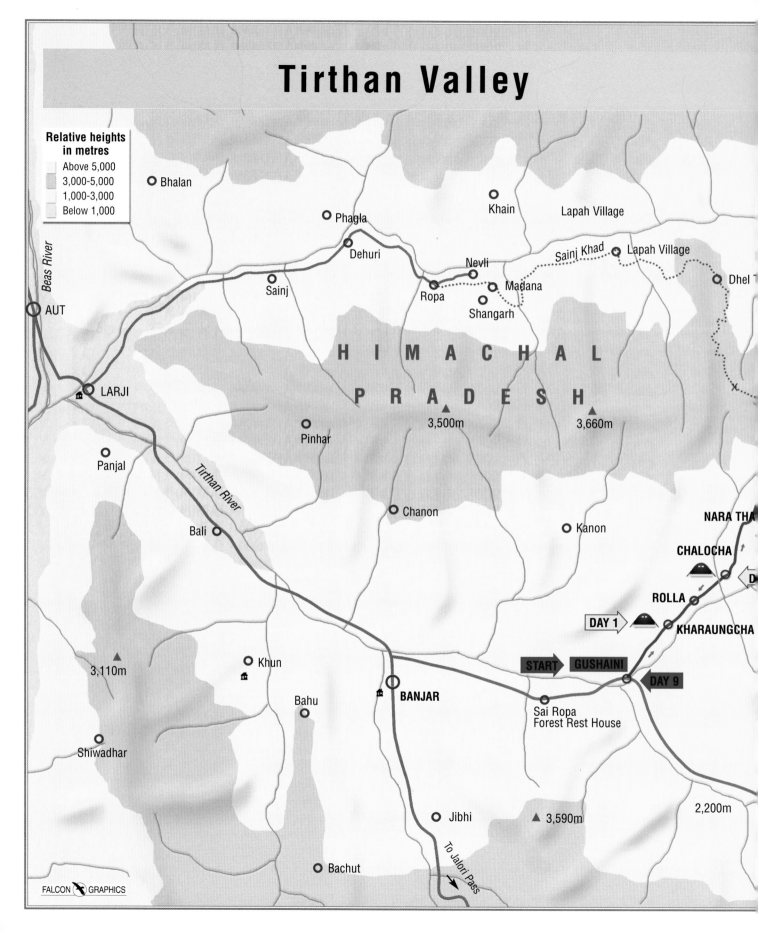

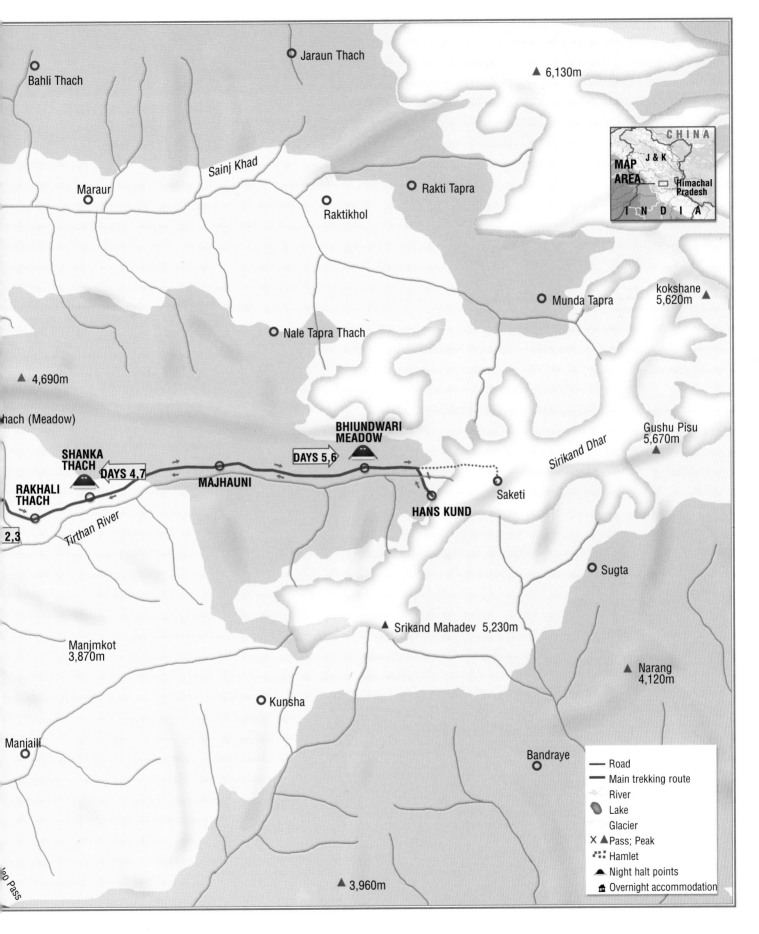

Bahli Thach

Jaraun Thach

▲ 6,130m

Sainj Khad

Maraur

Rakti Tapra

Raktikhol

Munda Tapra

kokshane
5,620m ▲

Nale Tapra Thach

▲ 4,690m

hach (Meadow)

BHIUNDWARI
MEADOW

Gushu Pisu
5,670m
▲

SHANKA
THACH

DAYS 4,7

DAYS 5,6

Sirikand Dhar

RAKHALI
THACH

MAJHAUNI

Saketi

2,3

Tirthan River

HANS KUND

Sugta

Srikand Mahadev 5,230m

Manjmkot
3,870m

Narang
4,120m

Kunsha

Manjaili

Bandraye

⌐0 Pass

▲ 3,960m

	Road
	Main trekking route
	River
◗	Lake
	Glacier
✕ ▲	Pass; Peak
⋮⋮⋮	Hamlet
▲	Night halt points
⌂	Overnight accommodation

CHINA

J & K

MAP
AREA

Himachal
Pradesh

I N D I A

built animal sporting a shaggy coat of hair and curving horns. Another goat species found on the cliff sides is the goral, smaller than the tahr. Its loud hisses can be heard at a distance. If you hear whistling screams followed by snorts, then you can be sure a herd of serows is grazing nearby. Another intermediate between goat-antelopes and goats, the serow can be identified by the stocking-like lower half of its limbs. It is as big as the tahr.

Even the common leopard, on the apex of the food chain in these parts, is found there in summer. In winter, it retreats to the lower forests. An exploratory climb to the Kabri meadow (12,800 ft / 3,900 m) is highly recommended on this day. You could see the spectacle of the red giant flying squirrel gliding from one tree to the other using the parachute-like membrane between its limbs. If lucky, you could also glimpse the fabled musk deer foraging in the undergrowth. Come back to the camp at Nara at the end of the day.

■ **DAY 4**: The trail traverses the mountainside for an hour or so through extremely thick forest and then descends steeply to a small side stream. You can barely make out the path and may have to scramble down. Soon you are at the shepherd's encampment at Rakhali (9,500 ft / 2,895 m).

Follow the right bank of the Tirthan and then follow the river for an hour and a half to reach the campsite at Shanka Thach, 10,100 ft / 3,078 m.

■ **DAY 5**: A tricky trail over scree slopes prone to landslides, offers logs for the climber. A taxing walk leads to Majhauni, where the forest ends but the trail becomes deceptive. As the valley opens up, the route passes over scree slopes and ice patches to reach the Tirth meadow, carpeted with flowers, particularly *fritillaries*, anemones and *obtuseloba*. A short walk away is Bhiundwari (12,000 ft / 3,657 m) at the junction of two valleys. The name of the camp is derived from a rock shelter, a ten-minute walk from the camp. There Bhim, the Pandava prince, meditated during his twelve-year exile.

■ **DAY 6**: Camping at Bhiundwari, go for an exploratory walk to Hans Kund, the sacred pool from where the Tirthan originates. A forty-five-minute walk brings you to the spot marked by saffron flags. The locals never camp there since it is held to be sacred. The area around is typical snow leopard and brown bear territory. On the slopes around Hans Kund, you could see herds of blue sheep, an intermediate between a goat and sheep with large curved horns. Horned Ibex can also be seen.

■ **DAYS 7-9**: Now start heading back via Shanka, Nara, Chalocha, and Kharaungcha. At a brisk pace you can be back at Gushaini on the afternoon

Pretty girl who became a *devi*

THE *DEVI* or goddess at Gushaini was originally a pretty girl, the daughter of a Thakur of Dethua village. He once employed a local mason and impressed by his craftsmanship, promised the mason anything he desired. The mason asked for the daughter's hand and the Thakur consented. The girl went off with the mason to keep her father's honour but was unhappy with her low-bred husband. One day as she sat crying by the bank of the Tirthan, the river drew her into its cold waters, and she became a *devi*. Sociologists will tell you how society reaffirms its structural arrangements through myths. In this case, a transgression of the caste-based marital system and the unease of a Thakur who could not go against his word of honour, were taken care of by the drowning of the girl. Her reward: the status of a *devi* and a place in the local temple!

of the ninth day. An alternate but extremely tough possibility is to climb onto the right ridge of the Tirthan valley, descend to the Sainj, and then go up similarly to Jiwa and Parbati valleys. But this requires time, experience, technical know-how and a definite kink in the mind! An alternative route from Nara Thach takes one across the ridge to the Sainj valley over Lapah and Shangarh villages. Two more days are needed for this trip, but make sure your guide is familiar with the route.

■ Facing page: Women and children add colour to the mountains.

Trek V

To Bara Bangal

▮I Palachak meadow in the upper Uhl valley

There was a time when, in Himachal, information was taken by traders and shepherds trudging along steep unmarked trails between isolated valleys. Though traders today prefer the truck and the road, you can still hear the shrill piercing whistle of the Gaddi shepherd herding his flock.

▮I **DAY 1**: Reach Manali town by road or by air to Kulu and then drive up the last forty-five kilometres to Manali (6,221 ft / 1,898 m). Spend a day at Manali making arrangements for horses and buying provisions. On the first day, follow the Manalsu Nala, which joins the Beas at Manali. The trail stays above the river on its right bank for an hour and a half. Three hours of steep switchbacks through thick oak forest lead to a grassland half-way up the hill. The trail continues on a well-marked path that goes through a forest of pine, maple, and oak to reach the Lamadug meadows (9,900 ft / 3,017 m). Just after spring, the meadow is carpeted with flowers. But in autumn the grass is so high that it's difficult to find the camping site. If you have any energy left and are game for a nice scramble, then climb the Khandpara Top above Lambadhug for some lovely views of Kulu valley.

In the forests, there is a good possibility of seeing pheasants, Himalayan black bears, musk deer, barking deer, and the tahr. While on the cliffs, you could encounter gorals and, above the tree line on the left

Ways & Means

Duration

12 to 13 days

Degree of Difficulty

4: Moderate to rigorous

Getting There

Same as Beas Kund-Bhrigu Lake trek.

Best Time

May (snow permitting) to early July, and again from mid-September to end-November (or later if there is no fresh snow to block the passes).

Altitude

Manali at 6,221 ft / 1,898 m is the starting point of the trek, and Bir at 3,000 ft / 915 m is where the trek ends. The high points are two passes, the Kalihani at 15,740 ft / 4,797 m and the Thamsar at 15,171 ft / 4,624 m. The highest campsite is at Sangor at over 13,000 ft / 3,960 m.

Highlights

Explore the remote valley of the Gaddi shepherds that is cut off for most of the year. Walk through the Uhl valley, one of the most scenic of the Western Himalaya. See the Dussehra festival in Kulu in October.

Support Services

Many trek organisers in Manali can make all the arrangements. Pack animals are available in Manali if trek has to be organised on own. Be self-supplied for food and camping.

Emergency

Manali is the only place to get medical help or rescue facilities. On trek, the only communication is from Bara Bangal village and from Rajgunda village.

bank of the Manalsu river, ibex herds have reportedly been seen. If luck favours you, then a couple of days spent here could be quite rewarding.

■ DAY 2: The trail climbs up towards the Khandpara top. For the first one and a half hours it passes through a rhododendron forest and then through fir and spruce to reach the end of the tree line. In an hour you are above the tree line and reach a fork. While one path continues into the Manalsu valley, the other climbs up steeply for an hour to reach a saddle on a large sloping meadow, locally known as the Khandpara Pass (12,700 ft / 3,870 m). Incredible views from this spot — look north towards Beas Kund and you can see the summits of Hanuman Tibba, Ladakhi; Friendship and Manali Peaks; to the east across the Beas valley loom up Deo Tibba and Indrasen, and beyond it the Chandrabhaga peaks. Below, the Beas river runs through the Kulu valley. A forest trail for half an hour leaves the bigger trail to descend steeply for almost eight hundred feet on a narrower path towards the Dora Nala. After crossing the stream, traverse up the ridge for ninety minutes to a Gaddi camp. Go down to the path below and then climb up to the top of the hump. Now you are in the upper valley of the Beragram Nala. The valley narrows down and in another two hours you reach Riyali Thach (11,200 ft / 3,414 m), a large Gaddi encampment. At the head of the valley, see the Kalihani pass.

■ DAY 3: Traverse the mountainside, crossing two side streams to reach a

bigger stream, which is a trifle difficult to ford. On the other side, the trail climbs on to the right ridge to ascend to the campsite at Sangor meadow. This place could get terribly windy and cold, but on the flip side, you get a rerun of the views you got from the Khandpara pass and a lovely sunset over the Kulu valley, as the clouds turn crimson over Deo Tibba.

■ DAY 4: Head towards the grassy ridge on the right of the waterfall beyond the camp to climb on to a scree slope to reach the base of the Kalihani Pass. After fours hours of steep switchbacks, with the last forty-five minutes on snow, you reach the top of the pass (15,740 ft / 4,797 m). A big slice of the Dhauladhar range is now visible in the west. A steep descent veering to the left leads to three glaciated lakes that might be covered with ice and snow just after spring. Keeping to the right of the lakes on a gradual descent, followed by a steep drop, you reach the trail again. After a long march of four hours, you reach the first Gaddi camp of Nangor (12,800 ft / 3,901 m).

■ DAY 5: While staying on the right bank of the Kalihani river, the trail goes through scree and

**■ Musk deer

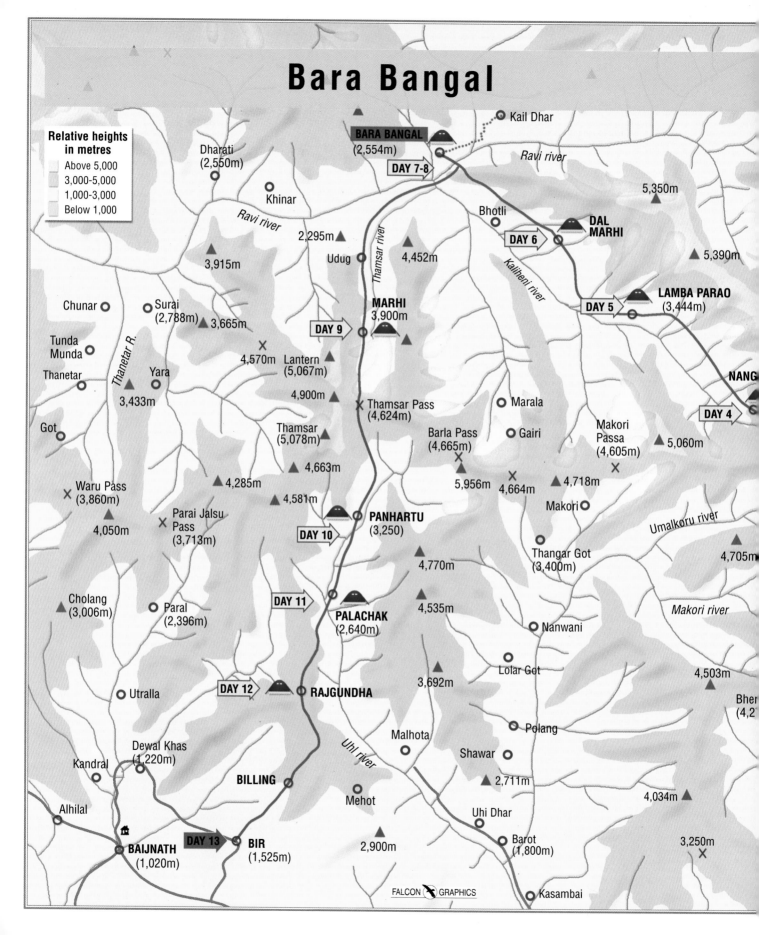

Bara Bangal

Relative heights in metres
- Above 5,000
- 3,000-5,000
- 1,000-3,000
- Below 1,000

Kail Dhar

BARA BANGAL (2,554m)
DAY 7-8

Ravi river

Dharati (2,550m)

Khinar

Bhotli

5,350m

Ravi river

3,915m

2,295m

Udug

4,452m

DAL MARHI
DAY 6

5,390m

Chunar

Surai (2,788m)

3,665m

Thamsar river

MARHI 3,900m
DAY 9

Kalilheni river

LAMBA PARAO (3,444m)
DAY 5

Tunda Munda

Thanetar R.

4,570m

Lantern (5,067m)

NANG

Thanetar

Yara

3,433m

4,900m

Thamsar Pass (4,624m)

Marala

Gairi

Makori Passa (4,605m)

DAY 4

Got

Thamsar (5,078m)

Barla Pass (4,665m)

5,060m

Waru Pass (3,860m)

4,663m

5,956m

4,664m

4,718m

4,050m

4,285m

Makori

4,581m

Parai Jalsu Pass (3,713m)

PANHARTU (3,250)
DAY 10

Umalkoru river

4,770m

Thangar Got (3,400m)

4,705m

Cholang (3,006m)

Paral (2,396m)

4,535m

Makori river

DAY 11

PALACHAK (2,640m)

Nanwani

4,503m

3,692m

Lolar Got

Utralla

DAY 12

RAJGUNDHA

Bher (4,2

Polang

Dewal Khas (1,220m)

Malhota

Kandral

Shawar

BILLING

2,711m

4,034m

Alhilal

Mehot

Uhi Dhar

Uhl river

BAIJNATH (1,020m)

DAY 13

BIR (1,525m)

2,900m

Barot (1,800m)

3,250m

Kasambai

FALCON GRAPHICS

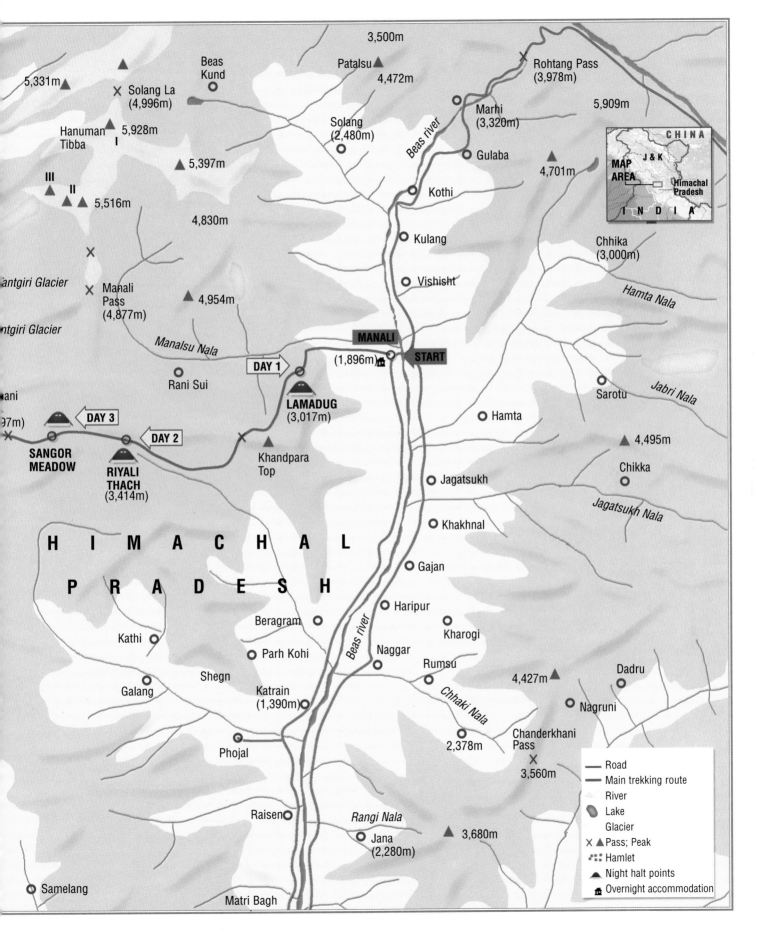

5,331m

Beas Kund

3,500m

Patalsu ▲
4,472m

Rohtang Pass ✕
(3,978m)

5,909m

✕ Solang La
(4,996m)

Marhi
(3,320m)

Hanuman ▲ 5,928m
Tibba I

Solang
(2,480m)

Gulaba

▲ 4,701m

Chhika
(3,000m)

▲ 5,397m

Kothi

III

II ▲ 5,516m

4,830m

Kulang

Hamta Nala

antgiri Glacier ✕

Vishisht

✕ Manali
Pass
(4,877m)

▲ 4,954m

ntgiri Glacier

Manalsu Nala

MANALI
(1,896m) 🏠

START

DAY 1

Rani Sui

Sarotu

Jabri Nala

ani

LAMADUG
(3,017m)

Hamta

97m)

DAY 3

DAY 2

Khandpara
Top

Jagatsukh

▲ 4,495m

Chikka

SANGOR
MEADOW

RIYALI
THACH
(3,414m)

Khakhnal

Jagatsukh Nala

H I M A C H A L

Gajan

P R A D E S H

Haripur

Kathi

Beragram

Kharogi

Parh Kohi

Naggar

Dadru

Shegn

Katrain
(1,390m)

Rumsu

4,427m ▲

Galang

Chhaki Nala

Nagruni

Phojal

2,378m

Chanderkhani
Pass
✕
3,560m

	Road
	Main trekking route
	River
🔵	Lake
	Glacier
✕ ▲	Pass; Peak
⚫⚫⚫	Hamlet
▲	Night halt points
🏠	Overnight accommodation

Raisen

Rangi Nala

▲ 3,680m

Jana
(2,280m)

Samelang

Matri Bagh

CHINA

J & K

MAP
AREA

Himachal
Pradesh

I N D I A

■I Glacier in upper Uhl valley leading to Thamsar Pass

meadows for three hours to reach the Gaddi temple of Devi Ki Marhi. Cross the stream, then another, and in an hour you reach the steep climb going up to the campsite at the meadow of Lamba Parao (11,300 ft / 3,444 m).

■I **DAY 6**: Traverse the mountain to cross the tree line. Descending for half an hour, reach the meadow of lower Khamet and follow the trail past two very old oak trees for another half an hour to upper Khamet, an enchanting meadow on the banks of a raging stream. Follow the trail for four hours, then a short steep climb and a traverse

take you to the Gaddi camp of Dal Marhi. A remarkably pretty setting for your camp, though it can get cold.

■I **DAY 7**: After crossing a stream near the camp, the trail climbs up for forty-five minutes to a ridge. A gentle up-and-down traverse of the mountain for an hour leads to Sunni meadow. From there, descend to cross three streams. A long traverse followed by a steep descent through farms leads to the Ravi coming down from the dreaded Tentu Pass. Bara Bangal, a permanent Gaddi settlement, is at a mountain knot where the Ravi, Kalihani, and

Thamsar rivers meet to form the Ravi's head waters. It flows towards Chamba and to the Punjab plains.

■I **DAY 8**: Exploration above Bara Bangal is the mantra. Climb steeply for fifteen minutes upstream of the Ravi and then for another fifteen minutes along the Nakori river. Now, a steep trail takes you to Kail Dhar meadow, from where you can see the three rivers meet. To your east, is Hanuman Tibba. Another peak is Laluni (2,000 ft / 6,095 m) with a lovely conical summit. To your south and west, the Dhauladhar range stretches out.

▐ The final ascent to the Thamsar Pass at 15,171 ft / 4,624 m

▐ **DAY 9**: Cross the Kalihani just above its confluence with the Ravi to climb on for two and a half hours and reach Udug meadow. After Udug, the valley curves and opens up slighty as the trail reaches lower Marhi. It goes around a waterfall to reach upper Marhi (12,800 ft / 3,900 m) in two hours.

▐ **DAY 10**: A walk on the scree or snow (if it's just after spring) for almost two hours takes you to a pretty lake at the base of the Pass. A steep climb in two stretches followed by a traverse reaches the Thamsar Pass (15,171 ft /

4,624 m). In an hour and a half, you reach the meadow of Bara Par where you could camp if there is no snow. Or descend for an hour to reach the tea huts at Panhartu.

▐ **DAY 11**: Walking through lovely spruce and fir forests and sunny meadows, crossing merry streams, skirting charming waterfalls and then making your way through more forests of oak and pine, you reach the Palachak meadows (8,662 ft / 2,640 m), in three hours Spend a day lazing or go down to the Uhl river.

▐ **DAYS 12, 13**: An easy descent through a dense forest interspersed with meadows for two and half hours takes you to Rajgundha village. From there the trail climbs slowly to Chaina Mandir and traverses the mountainside through a thick pine forest to reach Billing (7,500 ft / 2,286 m). Offering great views of the Kangra valley below, Billing is a popular take-off point for gliding and paragliding enthusiasts, and events are held there. A two-hour walk from Billing leads to Bir and the hustle and bustle of the Kangra valley.

▮I The stark mountains of the Ladakh Range near Leh .

7

Ladakh: The Last Leg

A FIRST-TIME visitor to Ladakh is struck by the economy of colours that marks its vistas. The valleys are green, the mountains range from brown to maroon, the sky is a deep cobalt blue with a few chaste white clouds drifting languidly. When evening falls, giant mountain shadows descend on the valley floors like menacing ogres.

Even the landscape showcases the ability to condense complex formulations within a simple cogent exterior – the hallmark of the philosophy, social structure, and physical appearance of this area. Behind every simple ritual, phrase, habit, or gesture lies a hidden meaning, the result of the dialogue between man and nature.

Geographically, the upper catchment area of the Indus river west of Tibet is Ladakh. All the water flowing down from the ranges enters this river. On this basis, it is quite easy to make out Ladakh's boundaries. To the north-east lies the Aksai Chin; to the north-west are the Hunza and Gilgit provinces of Kashmir; on the extreme north lies Chinese Turkestan; to its immediate east are Baltistan in Kashmir and the vale of Kashmir; in the south-west it's flanked by the Kishtwar province of Jammu and Kashmir; to the immediate south the Lahaul and Spiti regions, and spreading from the south-east to its easternmost border lies Tibet. Occupying almost 97,000 sq km, Ladakh is a part of the Indian state of Jammu and Kashmir with its administrative headquarters at Leh.

An intricate system of parallel ranges on both sides of the Indus valley defines the topography. To the extreme north are the jagged spires of the Eastern Karakoram from where flow the Shyok and Nubra rivers, forming the fertile Nubra valley. Rising up from the Shyok's left bank is the Ladakh Range that stretches from the Deosai plains in the west. Between the Ladakh and Zanskar Ranges flows the Indus. The Zanskar Range rises east of Kargil and tapers off as a plateau over Rupshu in south-eastern Ladakh and stretches into Tibet. The Great Himalayan Range marks the southern boundary, beyond which the monsoon clouds cannot enter, thus forming cold deserts in the north. As a result, precipitation in Ladakh is low and the snowline beyond 18,000 ft / 5,500 m. In winter

| The main balcony of the Hemis *gompa*

you could walk beyond 15,000 ft / 4,600 m, and people regularly cross passes above the Indus valley, some as high as 17,000 ft / 5,200 m. The air is completely dry and the proportion of oxygen quite low as compared to other places at the same height because of the lack of vegetation. But that has not deterred travellers.

Complex civilisations have risen and disappeared in Ladakh for the last two thousand years. Rock engravings dating back to the first century found in Zanskar and around Kargil suggest a link between Ladakh and north-west India at that time. Though Buddhist influences filtered into Ladakh from Kashmir, they were probably confined to the eastern regions. Bon shamanistic traditions held sway over most of Ladakh before a resurgence of Shaivite and Vaishnavite beliefs. These uprooted Buddhism from its land of birth by the ninth century. Guru Padmasambhava travelled through Ladakh on his way to Tibet and is credited with the establishment of lamaistic traditions in this area.

Following the drying up of the Buddhist stream from mainland India, Tibet started becoming important for Ladakh. At the end of the fourteenth century, Tsong Khapa, a Tibetan scholar, visited Ladakh to set up the Gelugpa sect of Buddhism headed by the first Dalai Lama. Gelugpa went on to become the most powerful sect. Ladakh became politically ascendant when Tashi Namgyal became the king of Ladakh in 1555. He unified the region and extended the frontiers into Baltistan in the west and deep into Tibet. Leh became the capital of

■I Making a sand *mandala* at Lamayuru *gompa*; below: Dancer at Phyang *gompa*

■I The statue of Chamba, the Maitreya or Buddha-to-come, at Tikse *gompa*

Ladakh. The Namgyals ruled Ladakh till the seventeenth century, repelling invasions. Ladakh became subservient to the Tibetans in 1685. The Ladakhis asked for help from the Kashmiris, who helped the king regain his throne, but imposed a regular tribute and built a mosque in

Leh. Ladakh's peculiar status as a quasi-autonomous region within Jammu and Kashmir goes back to the time when Zorawar Singh, the legendary Dogra general, defeated the Ladakhi army in 1834.

Owing to the slow obliteration of beliefs in Tibet, Ladakh has become the most important centre of lamaistic Buddhism. Located on the crossroads of trade and culture, people there are a blend of Indo-Iranian and Mongoloid features. Ladakhi culture has evolved into a graceful blend of influences, but it has not forsaken its spirit of Tibetan Buddhism. Gentleness characterises every action and thought. In fact, *schon chan* (one who angers easily) is considered an insult in Ladakhi. In a terrain that has limited resources, a system has evolved by which there are no sudden

population increases. For instance, only the eldest son or daughter has the right to family property. The younger ones join monasteries and remain bachelors. The population per square kilometre is just two, while the number of households per kilometre is .33. But, with urbanisation, Ladakh has had to grope its way into the modern world.

In Ladakh, everything is a celebration and in the folds of every Ladakhi *gomcha* (gown), you will find a wooden cup tucked away — after all, one never knows when one can be offered some *chaang*, the potent Ladakhi drink. Losar, the New Year (which falls in December in Ladakh), has celebrations stretching for a week.

■I Following pages 122-123: The village of Mud in the Pin valley, Spiti

Trek I   Shang La-Matho La-Stok Kangri

■I The palace at Stok village where the descendants of the royal family still live

In the cold desert of Ladakh each village stands out like an oasis. The availability of water determines the village's size. Channels of water designed generations ago still tap melted-water from the snows and bring it down to the fields. The cropping season is restricted to one-third of the year because of the lengthy winter. Over the ages, barley has become the fulcrum around which Ladakhi life revolves. Its flour forms the staple diet and it is fermented to make *chaang*. Animal husbandry supplements agriculture to complete the structure of the traditional economy. Animals provide transport, labour, wool, milk, and dung, the main fuel. Pastures high above the villages are dotted with settlements where a few members of a Ladakhi family spend the summer months with their sheep, goats, horses, yaks, and *dzos* (a hybrid between the local cow and yaks). The trek described here would make you experience a slice of Ladakhi life, besides taking you through a couple of high passes and to the summit of a 20,000-feet-plus (6,000 m) peak.

■I **DAY 1**: A two-hour drive from Leh takes you to Martselang (11,200 ft / 3,414 m), above the Indus river and close to the famous Hemis monastery. Descending from the village, enter the gorge of the Martselang river going away from the Indus valley. The trail criss-crosses the river through the narrow gorge. As it widens, you begin to notice boulders with small rocks stuck to them. These are conglomerate

Ways & Means

Duration
8 days

Degree of Difficulty
For the trek portion - 4: Moderate to rigorous. Stok Kangri climb -5: Rigorous.

Permits
A climbing permit, required for all peaks over 19,700 ft / 6,000 m, is obtained from The Indian Mountaineering Foundation based in Delhi. A fee of US $ 300 is charged and a Liaison Officer has to be taken along; all his costs have to be met.

Getting There
Leh is connected by air with Delhi, Chandigarh, Jammu, and Srinagar. Two high altitude roads lead into Leh, from Srinagar to the west and from Manali to the south, both involving at least two long days over several passes. Martselang, the trek road head, is less than a two-hour drive from Leh. Stok, the end point of the trek, is less than an hour's drive from Leh.

Best Time
June to September. Sometimes early snows by mid-September could make conditions very cold for the Stok-Kangri climb.

Altitude
Martselang, the road head, is at 11,200 ft / 3,414 m, and the highest campsite is at the Stok Kangri base camp at 16,500 ft / 5,029 m). The two passes are just over 16,000 ft / 4,877 m, and the Stok Kangri massif reaches 20,506 ft / 6,250 m.

Highlights
The chance to ascend to over 20,000 ft / 6,000 m without any technical climbing ability or equipment. Great views of the Indus valley, the Karakoram Range and the maroon-tinged Stok-Matho Range from both the passes. High altitude meadows with shepherd and Yak encampments. Shang monastery and village, so near Leh and yet so unfrequented by visitors.

Support Services
Pack mules and ponies available through Leh's trekking agents, but not available on arrival in Stok or Martselang. Other arrangements, including hiring equipment, can be done in Leh. Need to be self-equipped as no services are available on the trail. A guide will be a big help to chart out the easiest way to the top of the peak.

Emergency
Reasonable medical facilities in Leh, especially in the army hospital, including high altitude rescue facilities. On trek, however, there is no place to call for help, except that one is never more than a day's very fast walk away from a road head.

rocks — clay and pebbles cemented together by the elements. The trail climbs steadily as the valley turns south-west towards the confluence of Martselang with the Shang river. The campsite is next to a one-room monastery which was built less than two decades ago.

Houses in Shang village cluster on a slope with the trail passing a little below. A visit to one of the mud houses is interesting. Life normally revolves around the dark kitchen-cum-dining room.

The windows are small to prevent wind from coming in. Rows of gleaming brass and copper pots are kept inside a cupboard and the cooking stove is in a corner. Salty butter tea, *Suja*, is always available, though you have to develop a taste for it. Padded carpets line the wall and the place of honour next to the stove is reserved for the eldest person or for a guest. Low tables called *chogtses* are placed on carpets. Whatever be the economic conditions, travellers are welcome in a Ladakhi kitchen.

■ Stok Kangri Peak at 20,506 ft / 6,250 m stands guard over the Indus valley near Leh.

Shang La-Matho La-Stok Kangri

Relative heights
in metres

Above 5,000
3,000-5,000
1,000-3,000
Below 1,000

MAP AREA

CHINA

Jammu & Kashmir

INDIA

Khama Lungpa

Arzu
(5,087m)

Nang

Chumik

Digar La
(5,300m)

Pulu Digar

Sabu
(4,982m)

Siakno River

Thikse
Monastery

Nanga Sago
5,776m

Sobu River

Sabu

Shey

5,578m

Pulu

Fuchu Tokpo

Ganglas

LEH
(3,505m)

Choklamsur

Gomoki Chu

DAY 8

STOK
(3,413m)

Pitok
(3,284m)

Indus River

Stang-lha-khar
Fort

Lasirmou
5,570m

Tharu Tokpo

Tharu

Zinchan

Rumbak

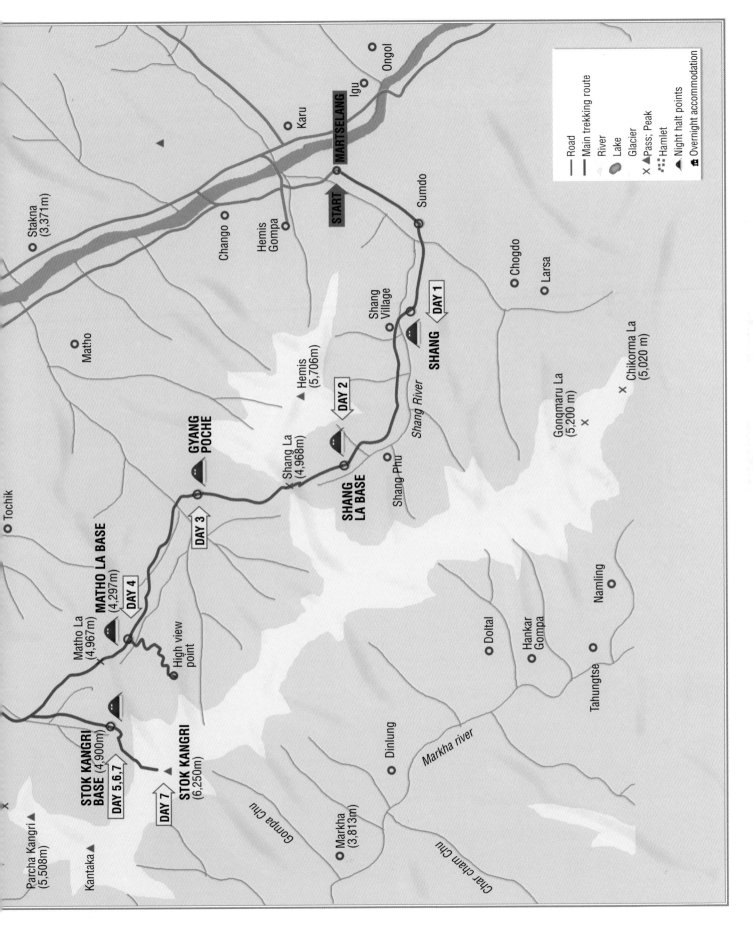

■I View of upper Shang valley from Shang *gompa*

■I **DAY 2**: The climb to the village is rewarded with a good view of the stone-walled fields and irrigation channels. Going down to the trail, start climbing slowly as the valley narrows. The trail becomes steeper as you make your way to the shepherd's camp of Shang Phu (13,900 ft / 4,237 m). A clump of juniper trees with a small shrine marks the pasture. Just above, the Shang Nala meets a side stream. Going up this tributary you reach the campsite at a junction of two valleys. This is a typical Ladakhi pastoral setting with small stone-huts called *phu-lus* that serve as summer dwellings.

■I **DAY 3**: Take the valley on the right from the junction where you had pitched camp the day before. Climb up past scrubs and wild rose bushes. Leave the stream to climb up the side of the valley, first laterally and then on switchbacks, to the top of the Shang La (16,300 ft / 4,968 m). The ascent takes around three and a half hours. From the pass, the views open up, with the Stok and Matho Kangri peaks in front and the summit of Parcha Kangri behind. A short steep descent into the upper Matho basin followed by a gradual walk takes you to Gyang Poche (13,600 ft / 4,145 m).

■I **DAY 4**: The trail stays high on the hillside. A three-hour walk on an incline, crossing side streams, leads to the base of the Matho La (14,100 ft / 4,297 m). As this has been a short day, you can go on a hike on the east slope of the Matho Kangri massif. A steady climb can take you as high as 19,000 ft / 5,800 m as you do not encounter any ice or snow. Across the valley are the Ladakh range and the Khardung La, and beyond that the lofty mountains of the Eastern Karakorams. To the east, you can hazily make out the Tibetan plateau.

▮ **DAY 5**: The steep climb to the Pass begins just after camp. On the Pass (16,100 ft / 4,907 m), the Stok Kangri looms up. Descend from the Pass to the pastures of Myungkirmo next to a stream. Leave the main valley and climb up westward to the left of the valley to the base of the Stok Kangri (16,077 ft / 4,900 m). The camp is in a basin with a lovely view of the massif of Gulep Kangri. Stok Kangri is hidden behind a ridge.

▮ **DAY 6**: Take a much-needed rest before you try the summit of Stok Kangri. In mountaineering parlance, a trekking peak is the name given to a summit that does not require any technical knowledge for climbing or any equipment for the ascent. But 20,506 ft / 6,250 m does require fitness and stamina.

▮ **DAY 7**: A long, arduous walk awaits you. Start before the sun is up. Climb up, switchbacking to the top of the ridge in front. A tough ascent on the mountainside for an hour from the ridge top takes you to the moraine coming down from the glacier. Climb up over the moraine for an hour and then cross the glacier to reach a basin in another hour. Now go up the east face over more loose rocks for four and a half hours to reach the east ridge. A gruelling ninety-minute climb takes you to the summit. If you go in August or later, you will encounter no snow except on the summit. From the top you get a magical 360-degree view of the whole of Ladakh — the twin peaks of Nun (23,250 ft / 7,086 m) and Kun (23,400 ft / 7,132 m) to the east, the Karakorams to the north, the plains of Changthang and the Tibetan plateau to the west, and the Zanskar range to the south. Descend all the way back to base camp.

▮ **DAY 8**: Turn left from the Mungkirmo pastures to follow the Mankyarmo river to its confluence with the Stok river. The trail follows the Stok river down to the Stok village. After the creditable feat of scaling a peak, you may want to look at some local history at the Stok palace. Or maybe you can go back to Leh and go to sleep in a hot tub.

Oldest monastery near Padum

SANI Gompa, a couple of hours' walk from Padum, is regarded as one of the oldest monasteries in the entire trans-Himalayan Buddhist region. There is a *chorten* or stupa dating to the first century A.D., of the time of Kanishka, the Buddhist king of ancient Takshashila, India. It is called the Kanika Chorten. Placed in an enclosed yard behind the assembly hall, its shape makes it conspicuous in an otherwise regular monastery. Another highlight of Sani is the semi-circular group of monoliths carved with unusual figures in a pre-Tibetan style. Sani probably stands on a spot considered sacred for a long time and had housed a temple when Shamanism flourished in Zanskar. The present building was erected in the time of Guru Padmasambhava, the Indian scholar of the eighth century. The statue of the great Kashmiri Buddhist teacher Naropa, head of the Nalanda monastery in Bihar, is also enshrined in a temple. Another short walk away is the temple and *chorten* of Pipiting. The huge *chorten* is built on the crest of an ancient glacial deposit and provides views of the entire Padum valley: To the north is the imposing rock face on which the Karsha monastery is built; Padum lies to the south-east; and the trail beyond leads into the Tsarap Lingti valley and eventually to Darcha; to the west, are the hazy silhouettes of the Sani Gompa; to the east, the cliff-top chapels of Thongde. To the north-east lies the gorge that leads to the ancient capital of Zangla. Inside the chapel is an impressive image of the eleven-headed Avalokiteswara, the Lord of Mercy. The Dalai Lamas are regarded as his incarnations and a pavilion has been built there for the visits of His Holiness.

▮ The prayer wheel is a ubiquitous part of Buddhist life in Ladakh
▮ Following pages 140-141: The abandoned *gompa* of Zangla

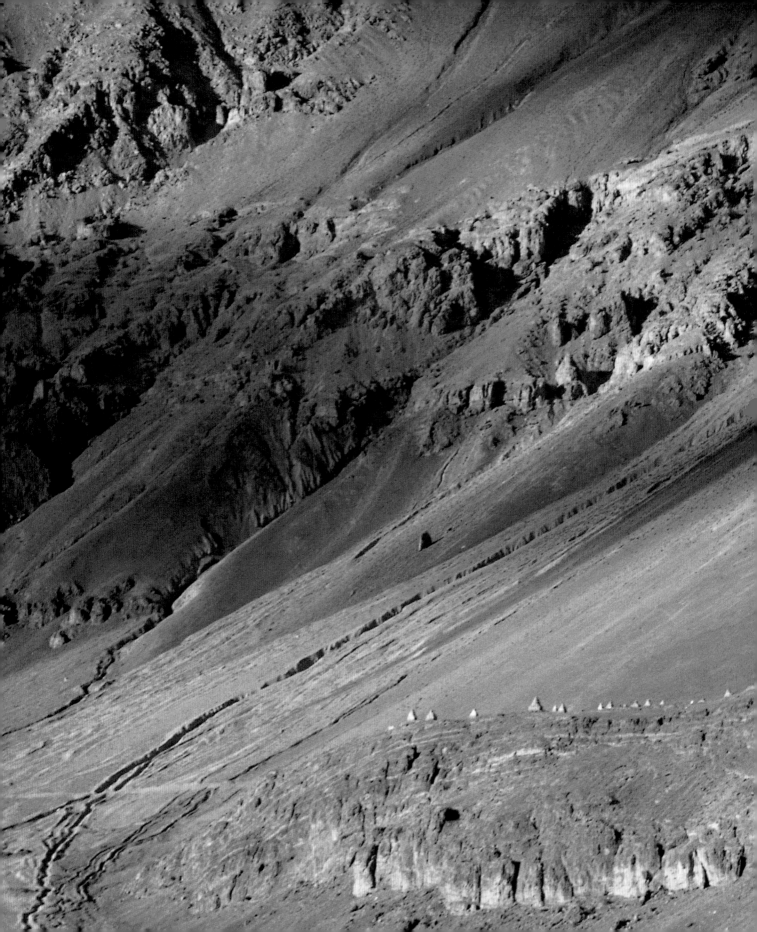

■I WIld rhubarb grows abundantly in Zanskar.

Trek II   ## Padum to Martselang

The landscape of Ladakh has been compared to the bleak surface of the moon. Images of the barren lunar vistas are similar to those obtained of this trans-Himalayan region. But its ecosystem is remarkably vital. Research over the last two decades has proved that Ladakh is the last refuge for the snow leopard and related prey species in India. The good news is that some trails take the wildlife enthusiast close to the wildlife.

The route that penetrates Zanskar from Padum, to Martselang on the Indus goes through a pristine wilderness. For almost seven days you do not encounter any villages, monasteries, or any other signs of human habitation. The trail takes you through a stretch remote even by lofty Ladakhi standards. Because of this isolation, it is an excellent place for viewing wildlife. With not less than sixty river crossings, the trek also provides moments of great adventure.

■ **DAY 1**: Reach Padum by road from Kargil or on the trail from Darcha. A short drive on a dirt track takes you to Zangla, the erstwhile capital of Zanskar, thirty-five kilometres away from the headquarters. The trail climbs through the village to the right bank of the Zangla stream and ascends into the valley. Clumps of willow bushes are found. With no permanent trail on either bank, you have to ford the stream at least twenty times. In around five hours you reach the campsite of

Ways & Means

Duration
9 days from Zangla; from Padum, 11 days

Degree of Difficulty
5: Rigorous

Getting There
Leh is connected by flight with Delhi, Chandigarh, Jammu, and Srinagar. Two to three days of driving via Kargil will take you from Leh to Padum. Another few hours of driving lead to Zangla, the road head. From Srinagar, two to three days of driving take the traveller to Padum.

Best Time
June to September. Care must be taken during the rainy season in July to cross the streams as even the scantiest of rainfall can make the water levels rise suddenly, leaving one stranded on the mountainside between two crossings.

Altitude
Padum is at 11,800 ft / 3,596 m and Zang La at 12,000 ft / 3,657 m. The highest campsite is at the Langtang Chu at 14,200 ft / 4,328 m. The three high passes are Charchar La (17,100 ft / 2,164 m), Zalung Karpo La (16,750 ft / 5,105 m), and Kongmaru La (16,900 ft / 5,150 m).

Highlights
Remote, barren and rugged landscape which is home to some of the best wildlife in Ladakh. Spectacular rock formations and clear blue mountain streams are irresistibly attractive. The steep passes, deep gorges, and several river crossings make it one of the most difficult treks in this book. High adventure is the name of the game!

Support Services
Basic food provisions and pack ponies and mules can be arranged at Padum. No other facilities are available on the trail. Be self-contained for the trip; food and camping provisions must be carried from Leh. A guide is a must. Trails are not well maintained and can be washed away. Muleteers may have to be offered higher fees for the pack animals as incentive.

Emergency
Only basic medical facilities are found in Padum. Leh is the only place that has some better facilities. No communication after Padum from the trail. Rescue facilities are possible but very hard to arrange.

▌ *Bharal* or blue sheep

Zumlung Sumdo (12,400 ft / 3,780 m) in a small clearing by the confluence of the Zangla with a side stream.

▌ **DAY 2**: The climb begins just after the confluence on the left of the valley. A two-hour ascent takes you to the point where the switchbacks begin and a three-hour climb takes you to Charchar La (17,094 ft / 5,210 m), marked by a *chorten*. The descent from the pass takes you on a gradual slope till the trail meets the Zumling stream. In little short of an hour the river enters a deep gorge. The gorge is so narrow that the ponies have to be unloaded. Sometimes, the drop on the cliffs on either side is so sharp that the trail disappears and you have to walk through the stream for almost half a kilometre. If it has rained, cool your heels and wait for the stream waters to recede. Battling this obstacle course, the trail reaches the campsite at Taktok Sumdo (13,900 ft / 4,237 m) just beyond the confluence of the Zumling with a side stream. The hill across the side stream is an excellent spot for viewing the ibex. Another animal not very difficult to sight is the blue sheep.

▌ **DAY 3**: Follow the Zumling downstream after leaving camp. The hills on either side are covered with willow; that makes it difficult to move on the trail, forcing you to cross the river occasionally. As Zumling is a

Padum-Martselang

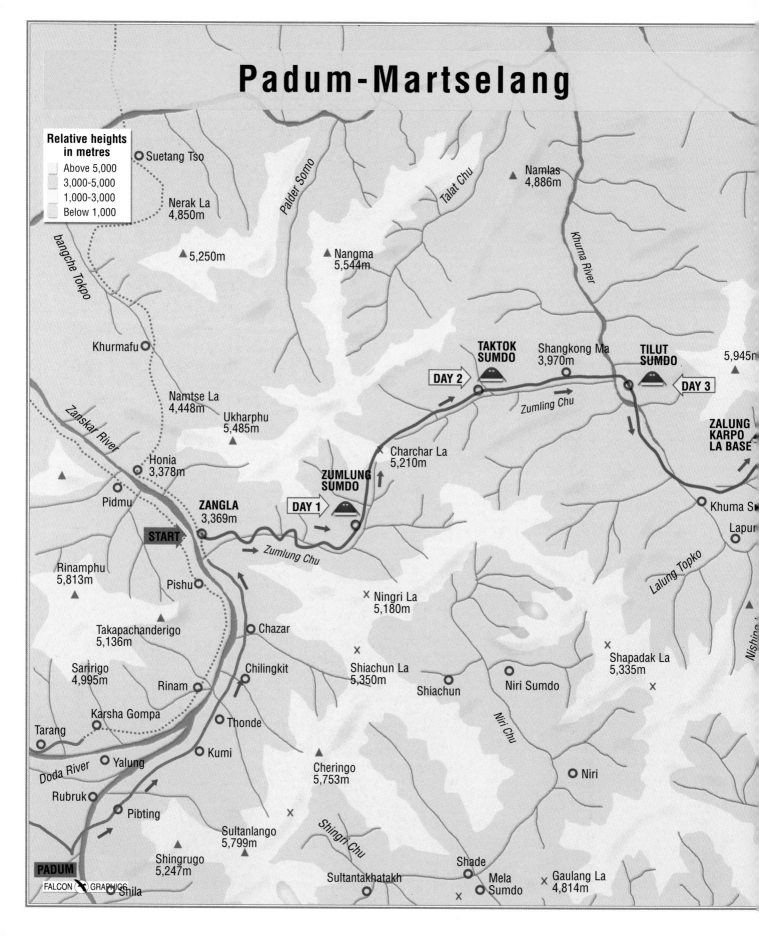

Relative heights in metres
- Above 5,000
- 3,000-5,000
- 1,000-3,000
- Below 1,000

Suetang Tso

Nerak La 4,850m

▲ 5,250m

Palder Somo

Talat Chu

▲ Namlas 4,886m

Khurna River

bangche Tokpo

Khurmafu

▲ Nangma 5,544m

Namtse La 4,448m

Ukharphu 5,485m

TAKTOK SUMDO

Shangkong Ma 3,970m

TILUT SUMDO

▲ 5,945m

DAY 2

DAY 3

Zanskar River

Honia 3,378m

Charchar La 5,210m

Zumling Chu

ZALUNG KARPO LA BASE

Pidmu

ZUMLUNG SUMDO

ZANGLA 3,369m

DAY 1

Khuma S

Lapur

START

Zumling Chu

Rinamphu 5,813m

Pishu

× Ningri La 5,180m

Lalung Topko

Nishing

Chazar

Takapachanderigo 5,136m

Chilingkit

× Shiachun La 5,350m

× Shapadak La 5,335m

Saririgo 4,995m

Rinam

Shiachun

○ Niri Sumdo

×

Karsha Gompa

Thonde

Niri Chu

Tarang

Kumi

▲ Cheringo 5,753m

○ Niri

Doda River

Yalung

Rubruk

Pibting

×

Shingri Chu

Sultanlango 5,799m

PADUM

Shingrugo 5,247m

Sultantakhatakh

Shade

Mela Sumdo

× Gaulang La 4,814m

FALCON GRAPHICS

Shila

×

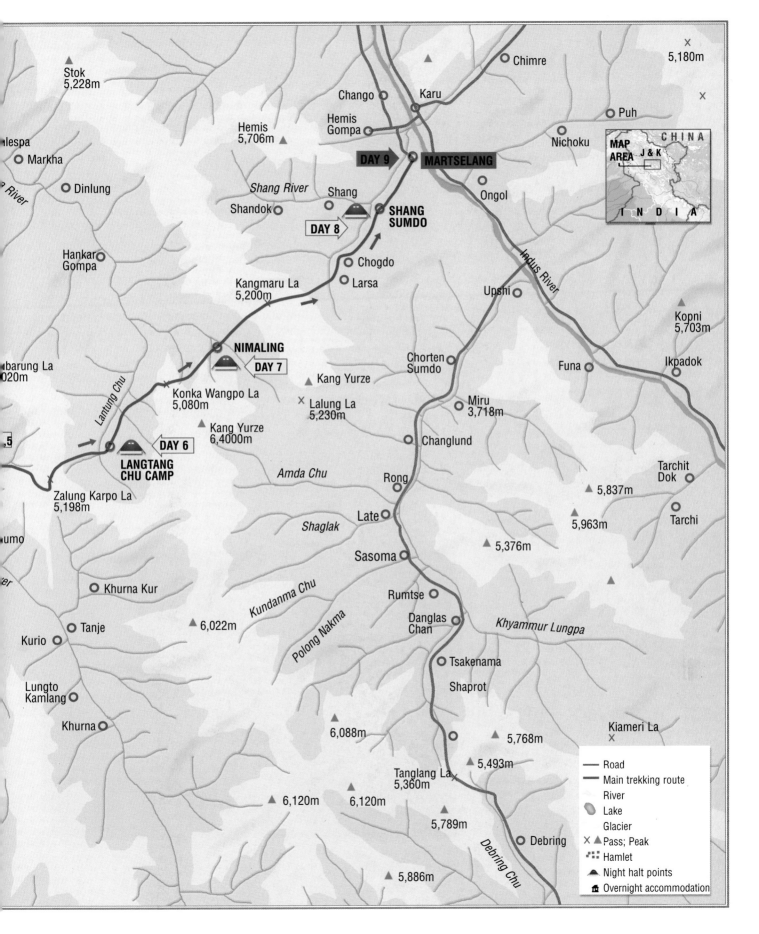

fast-flowing river, use a rope to cross the stream. In six hours, reach the confluence of Zumling with the Khurna. Cross it to reach the campsite of Tilut Sumdo (12,500 ft / 3,810 m) on a ledge just above the camp. This day's trek is through a gorge and you have to look straight up to see the sky. All sounds, even footsteps, echo eerily.

▮ DAYS 4-5: Follow the Khurna upstream on its right bank. The trail shifts to the left bank within forty-five minutes as the river comes down to hit against the mountain and swerves left. The crossing is difficult. Cross back to the right bank in another forty-five minutes and after a thirty-minute walk, leave the Khurna to enter a side valley. The trail climbs steeply through the gorge and it's a bit of a scramble when it disappears. But the valley starts widening and after two hours, the trail reaches a fork where two streams meet. Take the right stream up for three hours to reach the campsite. Rest the next day; explore the meadows for ibex and *bharal*.

▮ DAY 6: Leave camp early to cross Zalung Karpo La later in the morning. The trail climbs up the valley as it curves right and reaches the confluence of the streams descending from the Rubarung and Zalung Karpo Passes. The trail over the former goes into the Markha valley. Following the trail, going into the valley on the right, you reach switchbacks climbing to a huge slope. The ascent leads to the Zalung Karpo La (17,055 ft / 5,198 m). To your immediate east is the Kang Yurze Peak (21,000 ft / 6,400 m), and

beyond that, across the Indus, are the Ladakh range and the Eastern Karakorams. Behind you are the Nun and Kun. Avoiding the trail going down from the pass, take the ridge on the left for fifteen minutes to reach some prayer flags. Descend steeply on the trail, following a stream on its right bank till it meets another small stream. Climbing down a broad valley, a steep descent takes you to the campsite on Langtang Chu (14,200 ft / 4,328 m).

▮ DAY 7: An hour after leaving the camp you reach a *mane* wall where the trail bifurcates. Take the one going up, climbing steeply to the west ridge of the Kang Yurze with cairns and flags that mark the Konka Wangpo La at 16,667 ft / 5,080 m, and descend to a valley. Climbing and descending and crossing streams, you reach Nimaling meadow at the base of the Kangmaru La. This is one of the largest high-altitude pastures in Ladakh.

▮ DAY 8: Long switchbacks take you to the top of Kangmaru La (16,706 ft / 5,200 m), the Pass of Red Clay. There are ochre and maroon-coloured hills around. The Eastern Karakorams are clearer from this point, with the Saser Kangri's summit dominating the range. A sharp descent takes you down to the head of the Martselang stream – another great area for viewing blue sheep. A long walk through a dramatic gorge and then an open valley takes you to the campsite at Shang Sumdo.

▮ DAY 9: A short walk along the Martselang stream takes you to Indus's banks. Alternatively vehicles can be brought up to Sumdo for the drive to Martselang over a rough road. You have fared well on a tough trek and maybe seen some rare wildlife too. Time now to reflect over those cold river crossings next to a warm fire.

▮ Villagers from Zangla

Ways & Means

Duration
11 days

Degree of Difficulty
5: Rigorous

Getting There
Regular flights connect Delhi, Srinagar, and Chandigarh with Leh. Roads link Manali and Srinagar with Leh. If coming from Srinagar or Leh, leave the road at Kargil for a long day's drive over the Pensi La (open from early July) to Padum. Also, walk from Darcha to Padum.

Best Time
June to September. In June, Pensi La may not be open to vehicular traffic. Cross the pass (13,500 ft / 4,115 m) by foot and walk to Padum (three days). In September, early snows could again block the Pensi La. Otherwise, this pass is open up to mid-end-October.

Altitude
The heights of the high passes are: Haluma La (16,400 ft / 5,000 m); Singi La (16,600 ft / 5,060 m); Sirsir La (16,200 ft / 4,940 m). Most walking is between 11,000 ft and 13,000 ft or 3,350 m and 4,000 m.

Highlights
Monasteries at Karsha, Lingshet, and Lamayuru. Great trans-Himalayan views from the top of the Sirsir La.

Support Services
Pack mules and ponies at Padum. Food and lodging at Padum, Karsha, Lingshet *gompa*, Wanla, and Lamayuru.

Emergency
Radio contact only at Padum. Only basic medical facilities at Padum.

Trek III

The Padum-Lamayuru trek, besides passing through fascinating Zanskari terrain, allows you to observe monastic life in solitary places. The monasteries provide a rare glimpse of sacred traditions as you go up the Zanskar river valley.

Driving up through the Suru valley from Kargil over Pensi La and down the Stod valley, you reach Padum, the administrative headquarters of Zanskar. Spend at least two days to acclimatise, fix horses, and visit the monasteries.

■ **DAY 1**: A leisurely two-hour walk takes you to Karsha village at the foot of the largest and probably the grandest monastery on an awe-inspiring setting of cliffs. Before climbing to the main building, a visit to the nearby Avalokiteswara temple is a must. Situated beneath the ruins of a fort, the Chukshik-jal temple is now a part of a 500-year-old nunnery. Its main statue of the eleven-headed deity is framed by monsters and a winged *garuda* (a mythological Indian bird). Carved out on a *chorten* are the terracotta statues of Buddha and Maitreya with typically Greek curly hair and straight noses. Another chapel, at the foot of the Karsha monastery is built around a fascinating fifteen-foot standing figure of Maitreya carved in the rock face. These carvings are believed to be from the pre-Tibetan times of Kanishka's reign.

Padum-Lamayuru

The climb to the main monastery zigzags up under *chortens* and through tunnels inside buildings which branch off into the monks' quarters. At the top, two main buildings are set on either corner of a large courtyard. The main assembly hall houses the library of scriptures. A fearsome figure of Dorje-Jigchet or Vajra-Bhairava, a demoniacal from of the Buddha, is the highlight of the hall. Sporting hundreds of arms and adorned with terrifying faces, the deity manifests the influence of Tantric practices on Tibetan Buddhism. It is much revered by the Gelug-pa sect. Another interesting image is that of Avalokiteswara, a veiled life-size figure. Descending from the monastery, a short walk takes you to the campsite on Stod river (also known as Doda) near Ulang village.

■ **DAY 2**: The trail moves on flat dusty plains and in three hours, you reach Rinam village. On the way, the Doda meets the Tsarap Lingti to form the Zanskar river. In winter, this river freezes up to provide an optional way to Padum on frozen ice. It is known as the *chadar* or 'sheet route'.

■ A Buddhist monk with a copper tea pot

Padum-Lamayuru

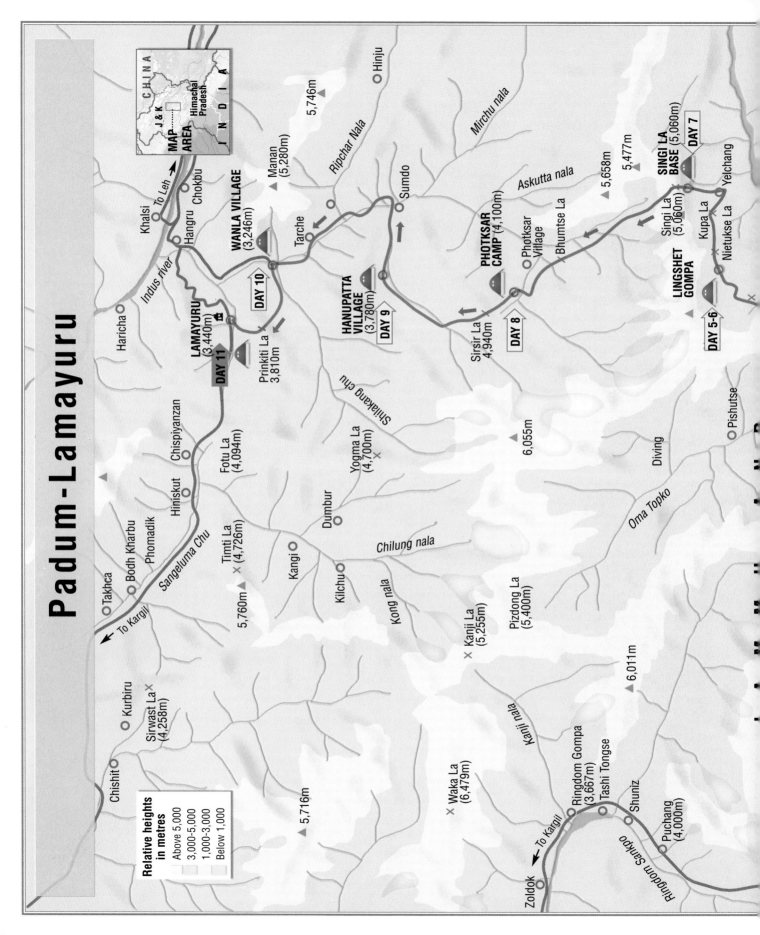

Relative heights in metres
- Above 5,000
- 3,000–5,000
- 1,000–3,000
- Below 1,000

MAP AREA

CHINA
J & K
Himachal Pradesh
INDIA

To Leh

Indus river

Khalsi
Hangru
Chokbu
Haricha

WANLA VILLAGE (3,246m)
DAY 10

Manan (5,280m)
Tarche
5,746m
Hinju
Ripchar Nala
Sumdo
Mirchu nala

LAMAYURU (3,440m)
DAY 11

Prinkiti La 3,810m

HANUPATTA VILLAGE (3,780m)
DAY 9

Askutta nala
5,658m
5,477m

SINGI LA BASE (5,060m)
DAY 7

PHOTKSAR CAMP (4,100m)
Photksar Village
Bhumtse La

Sirsir La 4,940m
DAY 8

Singi La (5,060m)
Kupa La
Yelchang
Nietukse La

LINGSHET GOMPA
DAY 5-6

Chishit
Kurbiru
Sirwast La (4,258m)
Takhca
Bodh Kharbu
Phomadik
Hiniskut
Chispiyanzan

Fotu La (4,094m)
Timti La (4,726m)
5,760m
Kangi
Kilchu
Dumbur

Shilakang chu
Yogma La (4,700m)

To Kargil
Sangeluma Chu

5,716m

Chilung nala
Kong nala

6,055m

Diving
Oma Topko
Pishutse

Kanji La (5,255m)
Pizdong La (5,400m)

Kanji nala
6,011m

Waka La (6,479m)

Ringdom Gompa (3,667m)
Tashi Tongse
Shuniz
Puchang (4,000m)

To Kargil
Ringdom Sankpo
Zoldok

FALCON GRAPHICS

X SuLabar La
(4,850m)

X Namtse La
(4,446m)

DAY 4

SNERTSE

Bangche Tokpo

Honia

Zangla
(3,369m)

PISHU
VILLAGE

5,136m

DAY 2

Parfi La
3,950m

Pidmu
Village

Rinam

Thonde

Kumi

START

Shila

Shilaphu

HANOMIL
VILLAGE

Rinamphu
(5,813M)

5,098m

Sasririgo
(4,995m)

KARSHA
GOMPA

DAY 1

Pibchu

DAY 3

5,533m

Tarah

PADAM

Puburigo

Trakkur

Burdun Gompa

Kong La X

Kyala nala

Detung

Detung

Tungri

(3,531m)

Phima

Lumur La

Rutagung La
(5,100m) X

Sani Gompa

Stagrimo Gompa

Shaggar

Zim
(5,288m)

Haptal Tokpo

Rulagang

Kangshu

Hamiling

Shagam

Ramala

Phe
(3,505m)

Tangar

Denya

Zonkhul

Sanchum

Mulung Tokpo

Gaura

Retang

Hutra
(4,910m)

Mulung
glacier

X 5,330m

Tepuk

Chibra

Hangshu nala

Klogaya Dost
(5,800m)

Ruhar

Haptal glacier

Chomochjor glacier

Boyo Comma

Trakkur

Chim Kurmo

Doda river or Stod River

Hangshu glacier

Hagshu Pass
(6,300m) X

6,100m

Bugjan

6,055m

Doda
(6,550m)

Chiring Peak
(6,100m)

Cimaltalia
(5,270m)

5,763m

Kange glacier

Banraj
(6,300m)

5,920m

5,960m

6,093m

Banraj glacier

6,000m

Pensi La
(4,401m)

Tso

6,050m

5,936m

5,710m

5,900m X

Road
Main trekking route
River
Lake
Glacier
X Pass; Peak
Hamlet
Night halt points
Overnight accommodation

In another two and a half hours comes Pishu village. The meadow below is an enchanting campsite.

■ **DAY 3**: From Pishu, a day-long detour can be taken to Zangla, the ancient capital of Zanskar, across the main river. Zangla was a kingdom of four villages enjoying autonomy within the buffer state of Zanskar. It became a separate state in the fifteenth century. Zangla is an oasis surrounded by desolate mountains — a recreation of the fabled Shangri-La. The imposing fortress of Zangla is now derelict and a neglected chapel inside houses a statue of Tsong Khapa, the Gelug-pa founder. The palace where the royal family still lives has another chapel with a library full of scriptures. There is also an old nunnery. Follow the Zanskar downstream. The walk

■I The cliff-side village of Photksar

goes past sand castles on the sides. In three and a half hours you reach Pidmu village after crossing a side-stream. A two-hour walk further upstream leads to the two houses in Hanomil. Camp has to be pitched beyond the houses next to barley fields. Large plantations of willow and poplar abound.

■ **DAY 4**: Within forty-five minutes, execute your first river crossing. For another one and a half hours, the trail follows the Zanskar river, climbing gradually, but punctuated by a few steep sections. The first series of switchbacks leads to the top of a hump from where the pass is visible. The trail moves on a long traverse followed by another series of switchbacks to reach the top of the Parfi La (12,960 ft / 3,950 m). A

fifteen-minute scramble up the ridge on which the pass is located leads to the edge from where the Zanskar is visible as it meanders through deep gorges — a terrific view, one of your last of the river on the trek. A fragrant species of juniper is also found on this ridge. A series of steep switchbacks takes you down from the pass to the Zinchan river in forty-five minutes. The trail leaves the river to traverse the mountain and finally enters a wooded valley teeming with willows and poplars. A short climb away is the campsite of Snertse. A thirty-minute walk from the camp on a high pasture takes you to a spot from where, looking almost 1,500 ft down, you can see the Zinchan river snaking its way through the valley to be sucked in by the mighty Zanskar. Right across is the Parfi La and all around are big bare mountains, some capped with snow. As the shadows lengthen, the mountains turn mysterious — a thrilling treat for a hiker. But turn in early because the next day brings the longest hike.

■ **DAYS 5-6**: The trail undulates on a steep path for almost three hours in an enclosed valley. The last hour to the Haluma La (16,400 ft / 5,000 m) is a straight climb up the valley's right. A *chorten* and prayer flags mark the top. In the distance, you can see Lingshet and its *gompa*, the destination that day. The trail is clear as it climbs up and down two smaller ridges. Nun and Kun peaks are also visible. After an hour's descent, the trail climbs up again to the top of the first ridge. In another hour and a half, you reach the

■I Karsha Gompa and valley

top of the third ridge opening up to Lingshet. The path trails down into the village and up to the monastery. The campsite is another ten minutes away. The next day is a rest day and you can use it to visit the monastery.

Lingshet is one of the most important monasteries of Zanskar and its main prayer hall houses statues of Buddha, Avalokiteswara, Maitreya, and Mahakala. It also boasts of a collection of antique manuscripts. The central figure is a wooden *mandala* of Avalokiteswara. The *thangkas* and wall paintings are exquisite. A new prayer room has recently been built with a large two-storey statue of Maitreya.

■I **DAY 7**: The trail climbs up and takes an hour and a half to the top of a small pass, Nietukse La (13,800 ft / 4,206 m). An easy descent followed by a traverse takes you past Yongma village and down to a stream below Gongma

village in an hour. In another hour, on switchbacks from the stream, reach the Kupa La. In two hours more, you reach the base of Singi La that is to be crossed the next day. The campsite of Gazo is next to a small stream.

■I **DAY 8**: A two-hour climb takes you atop Singi La (16,600 ft / 5,060 m) from where you can look up to the Sirsir La (16,200 ft / 4,940 m) and the valley in between. A short descent takes you

down to the upper Yapola valley and then the trail gently follows the river downstream. The trail goes across the Yapola and a short climb into a side stream takes you to a *chorten* and a *mane* wall in two hours. Crossing this side stream over rocks, followed by a traverse leaving the Yapola below, the trail reaches the crest of the Bhumtse La in two and a half hours. A descent from the Pass leads to Photksar village on the opposite bank of the Photang river. The village is on a cliff-side over the river, just before the waters enter a gorge. The campsite is a half-hour away.

▮▎ **DAY 9**: A thirty-minute climb takes you to a *chorten* where the trail turns to the right and the seemingly formidable ridge of Sirsir La rises up. The trail gains height to the base of the pass. From there, one trail goes straight to the top of the pass, while another goes right and takes a long switchback to reach the pass. The second one is safer. You are atop in two and a half hours. A short steep descent takes you to the valley on the right. Go down to the stream below and cross over a small bridge on the Spang Nala. It takes an hour to reach the bridge from the pass. Following the Spang on its left bank for two hours, you reach the valley campsite just above Hanupatta village.

▮▎ **DAY 10**: In an hour you reach Hanupatta set against the backdrop of a sheer rock face. The trail goes down

▮▎ The steep-sided gorge below Hanupatta village

▮I The mountains glow with the setting rays of the sun.

to the stream and then undulates all along the river. Soon it enters a gorge and after an hour you reach its confluence with the Yapola flowing down from Photksar. The trail now follows the Yapola downstream, staying on its left bank. There are three bridges that finally bring the trail on to the right bank. The valley opens up and the trail reaches Fanji La. In two hours, you reach Wanla village. This is the lowest point on the trek and the heat comes searing up from the path. The prominent landmark of Wanla is its ochre monastery. There is a dirt road leading out of the village and

joining Khaltse on the main Kargil-Leh highway. But taking that route would mean missing out on Lamayuru. For inspiration, there is a large supply of beer in the village.

▮I **DAY 11**: You can visit the Wanla monastery before hitting the trail to Lamayuru. It is one thousand years old. The main prayer hall houses an impressive two-storeyed statue of the four-headed Avalokiteswara flanked by two equally large ones of Maitreya. The wall paintings are faded and in great need of restoration. The room is shaped like a three-tiered mandala.

Despite the proximity of the Lamayuru *gompa*, Wanla is interesting in its own right. Leaving Wanla, a thirty-minute walk takes you to Shilla village. Cross over to the river's left bank over a bridge and ten minutes later, enter a narrow valley marked by *chortens* and prayer flags. A tedious walk over a hot and dry trail takes you to Prinkiti La, a saddle. A thirty-minute descent takes you to the fertile valley below. Lamayuru (11,285 ft / 3,440 m) surprises you with its mammoth proportions. You have reached your destination as have many generations of scholars, renunciates and ascetics, centuries before you.

Trek IV

Darcha-Padum

Ways & Means

Zanskar is known as The Lost World, The Forgotten Valley, The Land Where Fairies Congregate. A moral order built around a refined religious faith and a sound economy based on sustainable land-use patterns have created a fulfilling and comfortable lifestyle despite the harsh surroundings. The trail that goes up from Darcha in Lahaul to descend into the Zanskar valley is one route that typifies this.

❚❚ DAY 1: A long drive over the Rohtang pass and through Lahaul valley leads from Manali to Darcha (10,827 ft / 3,300 m), a nondescript village on the road to Leh. Starting early, a short walk on the tarmac road takes you to a switchback that climbs on to a dirt track going into the valley along the Kade river. An hour and a half on the track, and you are at the twin villages of Chikka and Rarig. The

trail takes another hour and a half to reach the bridge on the river overlooking a waterfall and gushing rapids. Another half an hour takes you to the camp at Palamu (11,300 ft / 3,444 m).

❚❚ DAY 2: Climb a scree slope, cross a side stream and go through a boulder-strewn stretch to reach the confluence of Kade with the Shinkun Nala coming down from the Shinkun La. Cross over to the other side of Shinkun on a bucket pulley, to reach the camp of Jankar Sumdo (11,746 ft / 3,580 m).

❚❚ DAY 3: The path climbs steeply for half an hour from the camp itself, switchbacking about 400 ft to a small grassy patch. Another four hours through a very rocky terrain on the right bank of the Shinkun Nala takes you to the campsite at Chuminakpo (13,320 ft / 4,060 m). A side stream meets the main Shinkun stream just near the campsite. Hit the sack early to leave very early the next morning. Otherwise, you will find it difficult to make your way on the melting snow.

❚❚ DAY 4: The trail starts climbing immediately after camp. The gradient is not too stiff but as you are at almost 15,000 ft / 4,572 m, the going is slow and tiring. After crossing a side stream, climb to the top of a hump from where the ice wall of a glacier is visible. The trail passes above the ice wall to the top of the pass. There are great views towards Lahaul valley. Trekking

Duration
10 days

Degree of Difficulty
4: Moderate to rigorous

Getting There
Daily flights from Delhi to Bhunter near Kulu (in the tourist season). From Bhunter, a two-hour drive to Manali. Many hotels there; stay for the night. From Manali, a seven-hour drive over the Rohtang Pass to Darcha.

Best Time
June to September. In June, Rohtang Pass may not open for vehicles due to the snow. Cross the pass (13,000 ft / 3,962 m) on foot. Buses and taxis are available for the rest of the journey. In September, early snows could make the crossing of the Shinkun La into Zanskar difficult. Also, the road into Padum over the Pensi La could get blocked.

Altitude
Maximum height is 16,700 ft / 5,100 m on the Shinkun La. Most of the walking is between 10,000 ft and 12,000 ft / 3,000 m and 3,650 m.

Highlights
Monasteries at Phuktal, Mune, and Bardun.Good views from Shinkun La and of Gumbaronjon Peak.

Support Services
Pack mules and ponies at Darcha. Rations available at Manali, Darcha, Purne, and Padum. A tent is a must; guest houses only in a few places.

Emergency
Radio contact and basic medical aid only at Padum.

▌I Phuktal Gompa, the highlight of the Darcha-Padum trek

from the campsite to Shinkun La takes around three hours. The trail leaves the pass to descend the glacier, initially on snow, and then it levels off to the left bank of the scree slope. After a gradual descent followed by a sharp fall, the path crosses over to the right bank across the glacier. Zanskar comes into view as you see the green meadows of Lakong. An hour's fairly level walk leads to a ridge from where a sharp drop reaches the valley of Tsarap Lingti. The last part of the walk before camp is full of beautiful flowers — the spotted Himalayan blue poppy, edelweiss, geraniums, asters, gentians, and buttercups. The camp (14,435 ft / 4,400 m), is set on the banks of the Tsarap Lingti. A large herd of ibex has often been sighted on the hillside across the main river.

▌I **DAY 5**: Use the morning to cross over to the right bank of the Tsarap

Darcha-Padum

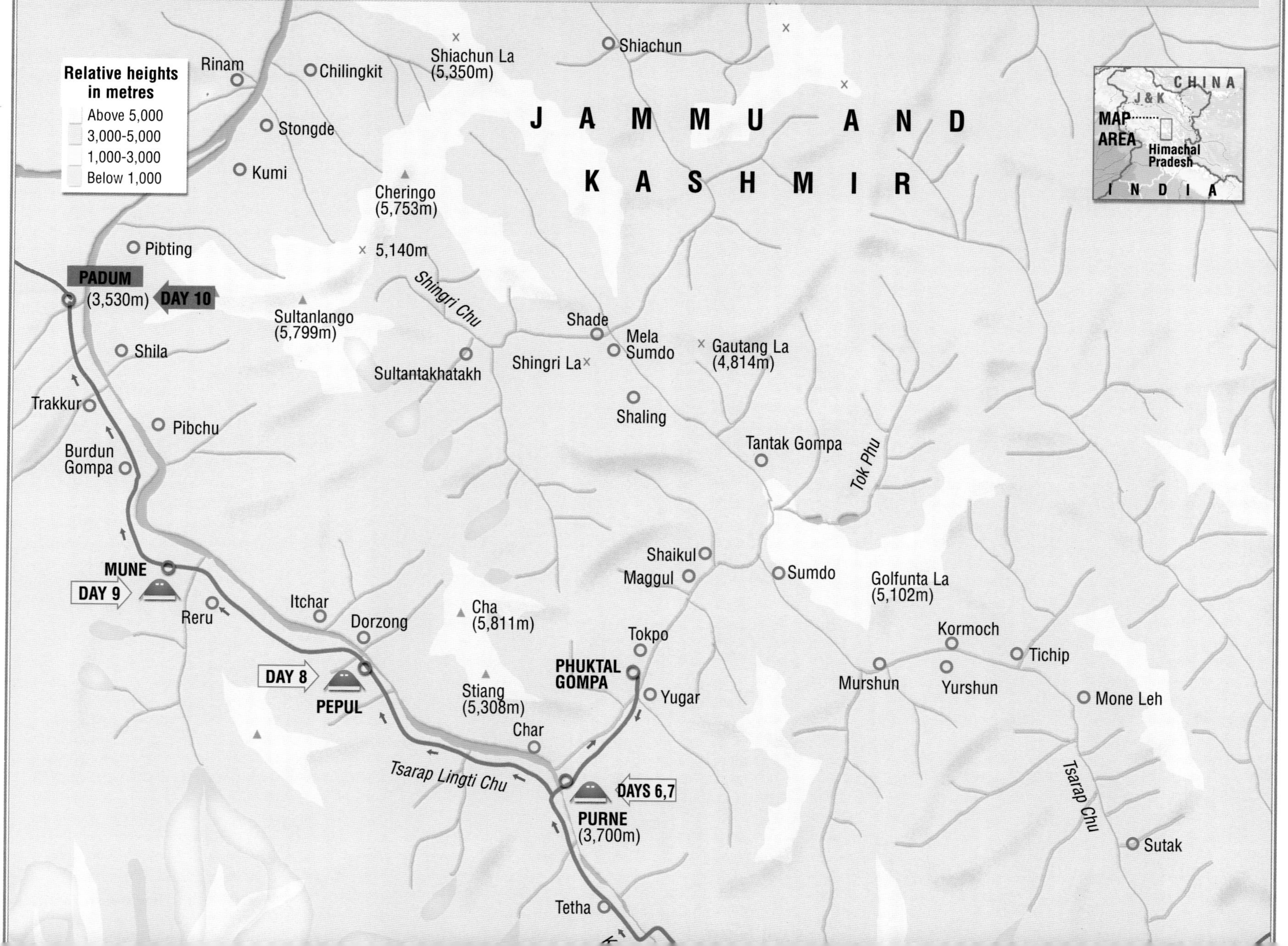

MAP AREA — J & K, Himachal Pradesh, CHINA, INDIA

Relative heights in metres

- Above 5,000
- 3,000-5,000
- 1,000-3,000
- Below 1,000

J A M M U   A N D   K A S H M I R

Sutak

Mone Leh

Tsarap Chu

Tichip

Kormoch

Yurshun

Golfunta La (5,102m)

Murshun

Tok Phu

Sumdo

Tantak Gompa

× Gautang La (4,814m)

Shiachun

Shade

Mela

Sumdo

Shaling

Shingri La ×

Shaikul

Maggul

Tokpo

Yugar

DAYS 6,7

PHUKTAL GOMPA

PURNE (3,700m)

Shiachun La (5,350m) ×

× 5,140m

Shingri Chu

Sultantakhatakh

Char

Cha (5,811m) ▲

Stiang (5,308m) ▲

Tsarap Lingti Chu

Tetha

Chilingkit

Stongde

Kumi

Cheringo (5,753m) ▲

Sultanlango (5,799m) ▲

Dorzong

Itchar

PEPUL

DAY 8

Rinam

Pibting

DAY 10

Shila

Pibchu

Reru

MUNE

DAY 9

PADUM (3,530m)

Trakkur

Burdun Gompa

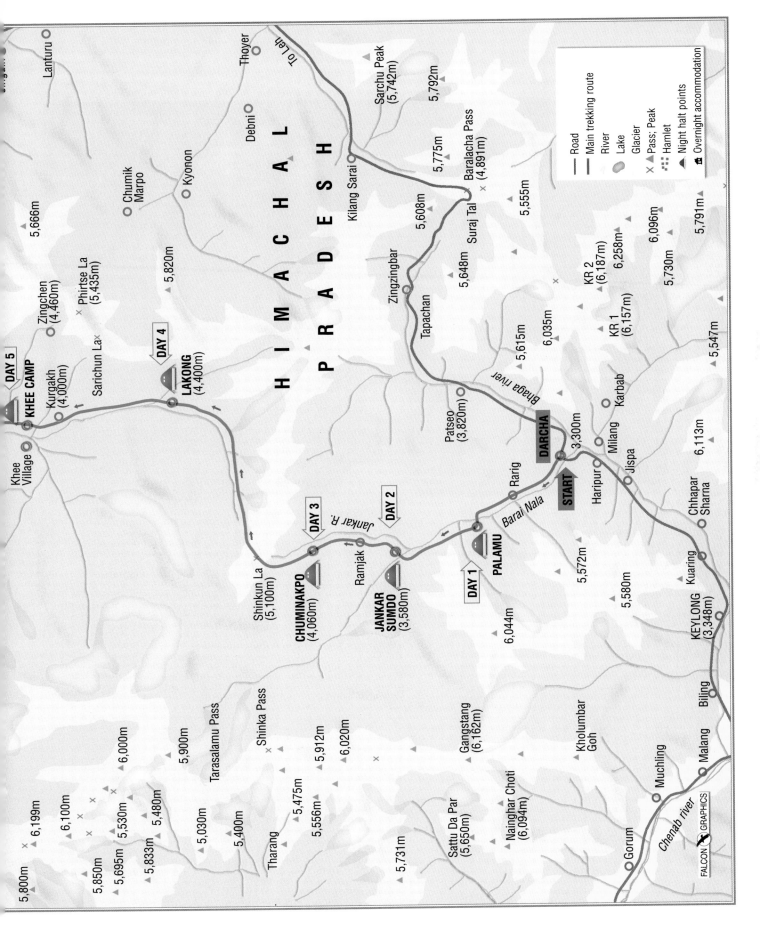

■| *Om Mane Padme Hum:* the Buddhist mantra resonates through Tsarap Lingti valley

Lingti. A gradual descent of an hour and a half takes you to the base of Gumboranjan, a solitary rock peak rising sharply from the valley floor. After thirty minutes or so you get a spectacular view of the rock face looking back up the valley. For a rock-climbing enthusiast, this would be an ultimate challenge, but the peak is considered sacred by the locals. In fact, the villagers believe a light shines on the summit on religious occasions. Well, faith is known to open up many a new vision for people. After a gentle walk of another four hours along the river, at times through lovely shepherd camps, you reach Kurgakh village. In

another forty-five minutes you reach the campsite at Khee village.

■| **DAY 6**: A three-hour climb takes you to a bridge over Tsarap Lingti, where the valley narrows down. The trail continues past the villages of Tabley, Shanze, and Tangze. Crossing over to the left bank, a short climb takes you to Kuru village. Another two and a half hours along the Tsarap Lingti past Teta and Yal villages, and you reach the campsite at Purne village (12,140 ft / 3,700 m), a small oasis surrounded by bleak mountains where the river Tsarap Chu joins up.

■| **DAY 7**: Keeping camp at Purne, go for a hike to Phuktal Gompa. The gorge along the Tsarap Chu is narrow with red cliffs rising sharply on both sides. The trail, at times, is quite narrow and exposed, and rises and falls steeply. You reach the bridge in two hours and cross over to the right bank. After a fifteen-minute climb from the bridge, you face the dramatic view of Phuktal on the cliffs above. It takes around twenty minutes to climb up to the monastery nestled at the entrance of a huge cave. Housing most impressive statues of Mahakala, the Lord of Death, and Avalokiteswara, the Lord of Mercy, and a priceless collection of

▊▏The village of Khee in the Tsarap Lingti valley; following page 160: Trekkers nearing the end of the trail

thangkas and frescoes, Phuktal is a gem of Buddhist culture.

▊▏**DAY 8**: Crossing over to the left bank, turn to the right towards the confluence of Tsarap Lingti and Tsarap Chu. An hour's walk over rubble leads to the rope bridge at Char, a relic from the not-so-distant past still in use. It's always better to see someone else crossing these precarious bridges rather than becoming a part of the spectacle – and sometimes part of history yourself! A thirty-minute walk takes you to Kyalbo village. There the valley becomes arid. It takes another two hours to reach Changpa Setin village.

Immediately after that you enter a gorge cut by a side stream. Descend a few hundred feet into the gorge; cross over a small bridge and then climb up again, and in another hour and a half, you reach the Pepul campsite.

▊▏**DAY 9**: An hour's walk takes you out of the enclosed valley and you start seeing the peaks of the Great Himalayan Range. In another twenty minutes you reach a bridge to cross over to the right bank, and then another hour to the fortified village of Itchar, with its houses clustered together. Climb to the top of the hill above the village to get a fascinating

view of the valley upstream and the snow peaks downstream. In another three hours, you reach Mune village where the camp is pitched next to an irrigation pond above the field.

▊▏**DAY 10**: Start early and go to the Mune and Burdun monasteries on the way to Padum (11,580 ft / 3,530 m). The trail is on a dirt track that tends to get hot. You reach the administrative headquarters of Zanskar in six hours. Take the road over Pensi La to get out of Zanskar or hit either of the two trails through inner Zanskar through a stunning terrain to reach the Indus valley in another two weeks.